D0772630

The History of Television

Don Nardo

LUCENT BOOKS
A part of Gale, Cengage Learning

Detroit • New York • San Francisco • New Haven, Conn • Waterville, Maine • London

LIBRARY OF CONGRESS CATALOGING-IN-PUBLICATION DATA

Nardo, Don, 1947-
  The history of television / by Don Nardo.
     p. cm. -- (World history)
  Includes bibliographical references and index.
  ISBN 978-1-4205-0162-9 (hardcover)
  1. Television--History--Juvenile literature. I. Title.
  TK6640.N37 2009
  621.388009--dc22

                                            2008053735

Lucent Books
27500 Drake Rd.
Farmington Hills, MI 48331

ISBN-13: 978-1-4205-0162-9
ISBN-10: 1-4205-0162-3

Printed in the United States of America
 2 3 4 5 6 7 13 12 11 10

Printed by Bang Printing, Brainerd, MN, 2nd Ptg., 10/2010

Contents

Foreword

Each year, on the first day of school, nearly every history teacher faces the task of explaining why his or her students should study history. Many reasons have been given. One is that lessons exist in the past from which contemporary society can benefit and learn. Another is that exploration of the past allows us to see the origins of our customs, ideas, and institutions. Concepts such as democracy, ethnic conflict, or even things as trivial as fashion or mores, have historical roots.

Reasons such as these impress few students, however. If anything, these explanations seem remote and dull to young minds. Yet history is anything but dull. And therein lies what is perhaps the most compelling reason for studying history: History is filled with great stories. The classic themes of literature and drama—love and sacrifice, hatred and revenge, injustice and betrayal, adversity and overcoming adversity—fill the pages of history books, feeding the imagination as well as any of the great works of fiction do.

The story of the Children's Crusade, for example, is one of the most tragic in history. In 1212 Crusader fever hit Europe. A call went out from the pope that all good Christians should journey to Jerusalem to drive out the hated Muslims and return the city to Christian control. Heeding the call, thousands of children made the journey. Parents bravely allowed many children to go, and entire communities were inspired by the faith of these small Crusaders. Unfortunately, many boarded ships captained by slave traders, who enthusiastically sold the children into slavery as soon as they arrived at their destination. Thousands died from disease, exposure, and starvation on the long march across Europe to the Mediterranean Sea. Others perished at sea.

Another story, from a modern and more familiar place, offers a soul-wrenching view of personal humiliation but also the ability to rise above it. Hatsuye Egami was one of 110,000 Japanese Americans sent to internment camps during World War II. "Since yesterday we Japanese have ceased to be human beings," he wrote in his diary. "We are numbers. We are no longer Egamis, but the number 23324. A tag with that number is on every trunk, suitcase and bag. Tags, also, on our breasts." Despite such dehumanizing treatment, most internees worked hard to control their bitterness. They created workable communities inside the camps and demonstrated again and again their loyalty as Americans.

These are but two of the many stories from history that can be found in the pages of the Lucent Books World History series. All World History titles rely on sound research and verifiable evidence, and all give students a clear sense of time, place, and chronology through maps and timelines as well as text.

All titles include a wide range of authoritative perspectives that demonstrate the complexity of historical interpretation and sharpen the reader's critical thinking skills. Formally documented quotations and annotated bibliographies enable students to locate and evaluate sources, often instantaneously via the Internet, and serve as valuable tools for further research and debate.

Finally, Lucent's World History titles present rousing good stories, featuring vivid primary source quotations drawn from unique, sometimes obscure sources such as diaries, public records, and contemporary chronicles. In this way, the voices of participants and witnesses as well as important biographers and historians bring the study of history to life. As we are caught up in the lives of others, we are reminded that we too are characters in the ongoing human saga, and we are better prepared for our own roles.

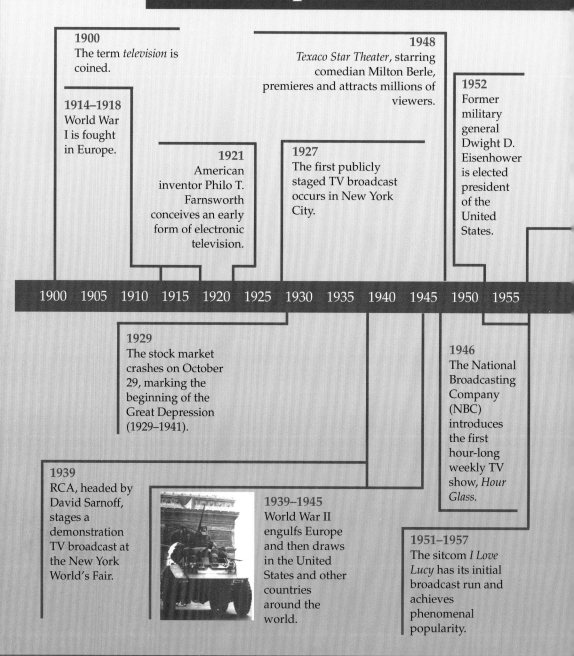

1900
The term *television* is coined.

1914–1918
World War I is fought in Europe.

1921
American inventor Philo T. Farnsworth conceives an early form of electronic television.

1927
The first publicly staged TV broadcast occurs in New York City.

1948
Texaco Star Theater, starring comedian Milton Berle, premieres and attracts millions of viewers.

1952
Former military general Dwight D. Eisenhower is elected president of the United States.

1900 1905 1910 1915 1920 1925 1930 1935 1940 1945 1950 1955

1929
The stock market crashes on October 29, marking the beginning of the Great Depression (1929–1941).

1946
The National Broadcasting Company (NBC) introduces the first hour-long weekly TV show, *Hour Glass*.

1939
RCA, headed by David Sarnoff, stages a demonstration TV broadcast at the New York World's Fair.

1939–1945
World War II engulfs Europe and then draws in the United States and other countries around the world.

1951–1957
The sitcom *I Love Lucy* has its initial broadcast run and achieves phenomenal popularity.

History of Television

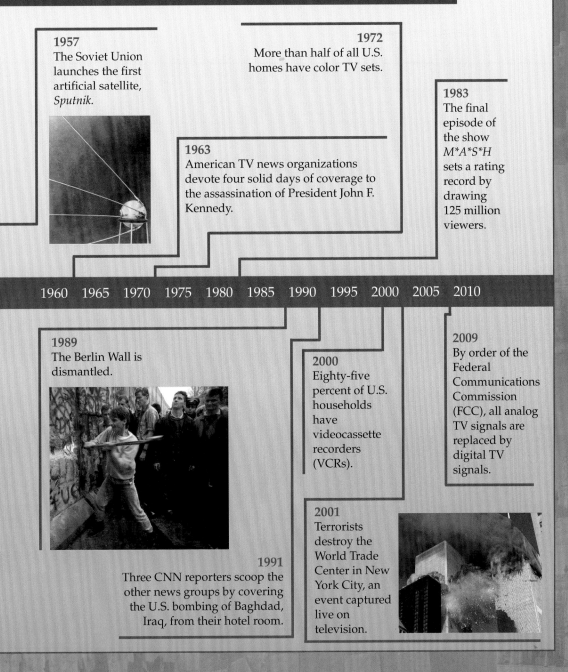

1957
The Soviet Union launches the first artificial satellite, *Sputnik*.

1972
More than half of all U.S. homes have color TV sets.

1963
American TV news organizations devote four solid days of coverage to the assassination of President John F. Kennedy.

1983
The final episode of the show *M*A*S*H* sets a rating record by drawing 125 million viewers.

1960 1965 1970 1975 1980 1985 1990 1995 2000 2005 2010

1989
The Berlin Wall is dismantled.

2000
Eighty-five percent of U.S. households have videocassette recorders (VCRs).

2009
By order of the Federal Communications Commission (FCC), all analog TV signals are replaced by digital TV signals.

2001
Terrorists destroy the World Trade Center in New York City, an event captured live on television.

1991
Three CNN reporters scoop the other news groups by covering the U.S. bombing of Baghdad, Iraq, from their hotel room.

Introduction

"The Air Has Eyes"

One of the earliest television broadcasts, in 1936, featured a song with these words: "The air has eyes that scan us from the skies, and ears that listen from the blue. So you needn't roam from your own happy home. The world will pass you in review."[1] To some degree these words were extremely prophetic. The medium of television did eventually bring world events, as well as national and local ones, into the homes of hundreds of millions of people.

Yet the person who wrote the song was unable to foresee the even more far-reaching influence that TV would have on a majority of global societies and the lives of their citizens. In a nutshell, television has changed these societies in profound ways. Focusing on the United States, Gary R. Edgerton, one of the leading scholars of TV history, writes, "America has profoundly changed since 1946 [when the public began to be aware of TV], redefining the way people conduct their home life, work, and leisure time." Television, he says, has also changed the way people "participate as citizens and consumers," and how they "understand the image-saturated world that envelops us all—largely as a result of the unprecedented reach and influence of television."[2]

The same things occurred, to one degree or another, on an international scale. Television "exercised an unanticipated and transforming influence" in many countries, Magdalen College scholar Anthony Smith points out.

Political life in democracies and non-democracies alike was thoroughly altered under the impact of television. A new consumer [buyer and user] society came to depend on it. In the sphere of culture it became the vehicle of the all-pervading Western influences of the [twentieth] century. . . . Television has imposed its own ways upon everyone in society who needs to communicate something to an audience. By 1990 in the developed [industrialized] world, 98 percent of homes had come to possess a television.[3]

Incredibly Accurate Visions of the Future

Smith's mention of "Western influences" is crucial to any discussion of television history. The TV medium first developed in the West, particularly in the United States but also with contributions from Britain, Germany, and a few other European nations. In fact, the development of television in these countries was probably inevitable. This is largely because it was the natural outgrowth of a number of technical advances that occurred in the late 1800s and early 1900s in these places. Once Western scientists and inventors had achieved a certain level of achievement in electronics, they created the telegraph, telephone, and eventually the radio.

These devices allowed people to communicate and hear sounds over long distances. But though they were viewed as marvels of their time, they did not allow visual images to be transmitted along with the sounds. Some people saw this as a shortcoming; they envisioned a day when it would be possible to broadcast pictures through the air.

One such far-thinking individual was French illustrator Albert Robida. In 1882 Robida produced several drawings of what he called a telephonoscope. In one drawing, the members of an upper-middle-class family sit in their parlor watching images of a distant war unfold on a rectangular screen. In another drawing, a woman chooses shopping items displayed on a screen; in still another, a young woman watches a professor teach a math class on-screen. Incredibly, decades before TV became a reality, Robida had accurately foreseen the advent of television news, home shopping channels, and educational TV.

Telephonoscope was only one of many names that early visionaries like Robida used to describe the concept of airborne images. *Electric telescope* and *audiovision* were two of the more colorful ones. The coining of the name that stuck, *television*, took place in 1900. It appeared in a paper penned by Russian physicist Constantine Perskyi, presented at an international scientific gathering in Paris.

The Right Place at the Right Time

In the years that followed, a number of other scientists and thinkers envisioned a device that would capture moving images from the air and display them on a small screen. Many of these individuals were Americans, which was not an accident. It turned out that the United States was at the right place at the right time for these dreams of broadcast images to come true. This happened as a result of several forces that were then reshaping American life. The first was the Industrial Revolution. The so-called machine age had begun in Britain in the late 1700s.

The telephonoscope, shown here, was one of the many names initially used to describe projected images.

But it expanded hugely in the United States in the late 1800s, giving rise to numerous new mechanical inventions as well as a keen interest and abiding faith in progress and technology.

Another force that gave the United States an edge in the creation of television was an urban revolution. The country's population doubled between 1870 and 1890, and large cities grew at phenomenal rates. "Millions of people were now centralized in an ever-expanding urban America," Edgerton explains. "Eventually they became the mass consumers who eagerly supported the widespread adoption of the telephone, the [spread] of big-city newspapers, the emergence of Hollywood, the birth of radio, and the imminent arrival of television."[4]

Still another force that made the early development of television in the United States feasible, if not inevitable, was a revolution in electronics technology and communications in the late 1800s. This period had "special importance," scholar Carolyn Marvin points out. During these years "five proto-mass media of the twentieth century were invented . . . the telephone, phonograph, electric light, wireless [telegraph], and cinema."[5] The advent of these new technologies spurred an onrush of creative thought. And that, in turn, led to the development of a sixth electronic medium—radio—

and then a seventh—the one that Robida and other visionaries had already foreseen—the transmission of visual images through the air and onto a screen.

As a result of these factors, the birth of television as a technology and art form took place mostly in the United States (although Britain also made some important early contributions). TV did eventually become an international, or global, phenomenon. But at least for a while, the United States (and to a lesser degree Britain) set the initial standards that other nations subsequently borrowed and adapted to their own situations. For example, scholar William Boddy says, "The flood of exported American TV shows that began in the 1950s provided models of program styles and popular taste for [television] producers around the world."[6] The major inventions and milestones that shaped the television medium are therefore inescapably bound up in the fascinating story of the American TV industry.

Chapter One

The Early Development of TV

Often new and useful devices are the work of single individuals. It is common knowledge, for instance, that Thomas Edison invented the lightbulb and Alexander Graham Bell invented the telephone. No single person invented television, however. Instead, as TV historian Albert Abramson puts it, television "is probably the first invention by committee, in the sense of resulting from the efforts of hundreds of individuals widely separated in time and space."[7] Edgerton adds:

Television as a technology is much more than a camera and a receiver. It is a process of conception, invention, commercialization, program production, and nonstop innovation. Television's birth involved one-of-a-kind inventors and workaday engineers, farsighted industrialists and bottom-line corporate executives, creative personnel and consumers adventurous enough to embrace this astonishing new technology and make it their own.[8]

These enterprising inventors, businessmen, and others would not, and could not, have created the television medium if it had not been for a few key precursor inventions. These were the telegraph, telephone, wireless telegraph, and radio. The telegraph, created by Samuel Morse in 1835, allowed people to send coded messages by making tapping noises that were sent through electrical wires. Though this was an enormous breakthrough, scientists saw it only as a first step; they wanted those same wires to carry human voices. Bell achieved this feat with his telephone in 1876. But again, some visionaries desired to go even further and transmit voices and other sounds through the air, without the need for wires. At first, this appeared to be a formidable challenge. But just eleven years after

Bell's triumph, Heinrich Rudolph Hertz discovered the existence of radio waves, a kind of energy that moves through the air at the speed of light (186,000 miles, or 300,000km, per second). Knowledge of radio waves allowed inventor Guglielmo Marconi to devise the wireless telegraph in 1895. And in the twenty years that followed he and several other inventors contributed to the creation of radio, which carries voices and music from one location to another via radio waves.

Radio turned out to be the most important forerunner of television. The first commercial radio station opened in the United States in 1921, and by 1925 millions of Americans had bought radios. Two years later, the government passed the Radio Act of 1927. It not only began regulating the radio industry but also introduced certain basic broadcasting rules that would later be applied to TV as well. One rule was that no person or company owns the airwaves. Rather, the airwaves belong to the people; so they can receive radio signals (or TV signals) for free. Radio stations (and, later, TV stations) would have to make their money by selling advertising time to sponsors.

Initial Technical Developments

Radio was also the most popular and widely exploited entertainment medium up to that time. By the 1930s, tens of millions of Americans gathered around their radios each evening to hear news programs, music concerts, variety shows, comedies, and dramas. Radio became a form of escape for the masses, especially during the economic bad times of the Great Depression, which held the country (and the world) in its grip during that decade.

The vast majority of people were so happy with their radios that they did not envision a more advanced device that could carry pictures as well as sound. Indeed, only a handful of individuals were aware that throughout the 1920s scientists and inventors had been hard at work on just such a device. Actually, it is more accurate to say *two* devices because at the time two fundamentally different kinds of television technology were under development.

The basic principles of the first, mechanical TV, had been pioneered several years before by German scientist Paul G. Nipkow. He succeeded in scanning the light reflected by a moving object, turning that light into an electrical signal, and sending it over a wire. According to author Laurie C. Hillstrom, Nipkow's device

used a set of spinning metal disks with holes arranged in a spiral pattern to scan the image. Inside each hole were . . . cells sensitive to light that, as the disks spun, repeatedly measured the amount of light hitting the hole. The cells then sent electrical signals that varied in strength depending on the amount of light hitting them. These signals were transmitted across a wire to a similar device at the other end, which reversed the process and turned the electrical signals back into light.[9]

Nipkow's cells were not very sensitive to light. His system, therefore, produced only hazy light and dark patches rather than clear visual images. But it laid the groundwork for later inventors, including an American, Charles F. Jenkins, and a Scotsman, John L. Baird. Working independently, they introduced mechani-

cal TV sets with reasonably clear images during the mid-1920s.

Electronic TV

Meanwhile, the second and ultimately more pivotal kind of television technology, electronic TV, was also under intensive development. It was based primarily

on an electronic device called a cathode-ray tube. It consisted of a glass tube with a filament inside, similar in many ways to a lightbulb. When the filament was heated and began to glow, it created a vacuum (an absence of air molecules) inside the tube. At the same time, a stream of microscopic particles, called electrons,

Families used to gather at night to listen to the radio, which paved the way for television.

moved outward from the filament. The stream was focused into a tight beam and struck a flat screen. The inside of the screen was coated with phosphor, a substance that glows upon contact with radiation, so the electron beam produced a bright glow in the front section of the tube. As a closed system, the cathode-ray tube created only that featureless glow. But when it received an electronic signal from a TV camera (or, later, a TV station), it converted that signal into images of people and objects on its glowing screen.

As happened with other aspects of television technology, no one person invented this entire process. A German technician, Karl F. Braun, developed a very basic version of the cathode-ray tube in 1897. Other individuals then expanded on and improved the device, including an English inventor, A.A. Campbell Swinton, and a Russian scientist, Boris Rosing.

One of Rosing's assistants, Vladimir Zworykin, moved to the United States in 1919. There, Zworykin took a job at the large electronics company Westinghouse and began cathode-ray tube experiments of his own. In the 1920s he developed a crude TV camera, which he called the Iconoscope. His bosses at Westinghouse saw no future for either this device or the television medium in general and ordered him to stop working on it. Undaunted, however, Zworykin continued his experiments at home, on his own time.

At the time, Zworykin was unaware that he had stiff competition in the race to perfect electronic TV. In 1921, while working on his father's Idaho farm, fifteen-year-old Philo T. Farnsworth, an avid electronics buff and mathematical genius, envisioned how a cathode-ray system might produce images on a screen. Farnsworth drew detailed diagrams of the system for his high school chemistry teacher, Justin Tolman. The older man was amazed that someone so young could conceive of such a sophisticated apparatus. In the next few years, Farnsworth built working models of his invention, which he named the Image Dissector.

Realizing that he was on to something big, Farnsworth got a financial backer and set up a workshop in Los Angeles. There, the young inventor conducted several demonstrations of the Image Dissector for the press and other researchers. One of the latter was none other than Vladimir Zworykin. It was 1930, and Zworykin had recently begun working for the Radio Corporation of America (RCA), headed by a brilliant, energetic business mogul named David Sarnoff. Unlike the owners of Westinghouse, Sarnoff clearly saw the potential of television and fully backed Zworykin's cathode-ray experiments. Of course, Zworykin, who now realized that Farnsworth's work was more advanced

Farnsworth Is Successful

Philo T. Farnsworth's friend and sometimes assistant, George Everson, later recalled a day in 1928 when Farnsworth was attempting to transmit a clearly visible image with his Image Dissector, an early form of electronic TV. The image was of a black triangle.

A square luminescent [glowing] field of bluish cast appeared on the end of the receiving tube. A series of fairly sharp bright lines was unsteadily [drawn] on the screen, which was about four inches square. [After the image of the triangle was transmitted] the luminescent field was disturbed and settled down with a messy blur in the center. By no stretch of the imagination could it be recognized as the black triangle that we were supposed to see. Phil and I looked at the blur with a sickening sense of disappointment. [But later, after Farnsworth had made some adjustments], Phil came to the door and announced, "I think we've got it now." [This time] a fuzzy, blurry, but wholly recognizable image of the black triangle instantly filled the center of the picture field. We gazed spellbound for a while.

George Everson, *The Story of Television: The Life of Philo Farnsworth.* New York: Norton, 1949, p. 89.

Inventor Philo T. Farnsworth displays his version of the television in 1929.

than his own, told Sarnoff about the Image Dissector. Impressed, Sarnoff offered Farnsworth one hundred thousand dollars for all rights to the invention. But the young man refused, saying he wanted to market TV systems of his own.

Sarnoff, who was adamant that RCA should lead the way into the television era, decided to crush Farnsworth. RCA launched a patent lawsuit, claiming that Zworykin, not Farnsworth, had been the first to build a workable electronic TV system. After several years of legal battles, Farnsworth won the case. He was now almost broke, however, and found that he could not compete with RCA's huge financial and legal resources. As New York University scholar Neil Postman says:

In a vigorous public-relations campaign, [RCA] promoted both Zworykin and Sarnoff as the fathers of television. Farnsworth withdrew to a house in Maine, suffering from depression, which was made worse by excessive drinking. He had a nervous breakdown, spent time in hospitals and had to submit to shock therapy.[10]

In this way, Farnsworth's significant contributions to the development of television were largely forgotten. He died in obscurity in 1971.[11]

Even before the legal battles between Farnsworth and RCA had concluded, an important watershed occurred within the then-small circles of developing television technology. By the mid-1930s, almost everyone in those circles acknowledged the superiority of electronic TV. Mechanical TV was largely abandoned, and electronic TV, which produced a clearer picture, thereafter became the industry standard.

The First TV Broadcast

Most Americans had no inkling of these ongoing developments and, in fact, had never even heard of TV. Only a relative few had seen the first publicly staged TV broadcast, which had taken place on

The Death Knell of Mechanical TV

Philo Farnsworth traveled to Britain in 1932 and there met with John L. Baird, a Scottish inventor who had developed a working mechanical TV system. Baird had no idea how advanced the younger man's electronic system was. When Farnsworth demonstrated it, Baird was crestfallen, as remembered later by Farnsworth's wife, Elma:

All the way back to the studio Mr. Baird was busily extolling the virtues of his mechanical system. [As] they came to the door, Mr. Baird . . . caught sight of the picture on the monitor [of Farnsworth's system] and became silent. He advanced slowly, as if hypnotized, until he was standing directly before it. He stood there for a time. Then, breaking the spell with a visible effort, he turned without a word and left. With great empathy, Phil watched him go, aware Mr. Baird had seen the death knell of his beloved spinning disc.

Elma Farnsworth, *Distant Vision: Romance and Discovery on an Invisible Frontier.* Salt Lake City: Pemberly-Kent, 1990, p. 166.

April 7, 1927. One of RCA's competitors, AT&T, staged the demonstration at its Bell Laboratories in New York City. Future president Herbert Hoover, then U.S. secretary of commerce, gave a speech that was broadcast over a distance of 200 miles (322km). Hoover said in part:

We have long been familiar with the electrical transmission of sound. Today we have, in a sense, the transmission of sight, for the first time in the world's history. Human genius has now destroyed the impediment of distance in a new respect, and in a manner hitherto unknown. What its uses may finally be no one can tell, any more than man could foresee in past years the modern developments of the telegraph or the telephone. All we can say today is that there has been created a marvelous agency for whatever use the future may find, with the full realization that every great and fundamental discovery of the past has been followed by use far beyond the vision of its creator.[12]

The small group of politicians and businessmen who watched this speech (along with a short routine by a New Jersey comedian) did so on a TV screen only 3 inches (7.6cm) wide. The picture was in black and white and lacked detail. Nonetheless, they were impressed that any sort of visual image could be sent through the air. The *New York Times* concurred, reporting the next day:

More than 200 miles of space intervening between the speaker and his audience was annihilated by the television apparatus developed by the Bell Laboratories of [AT&T]. When the television pictures were thrown on the screen two by three inches . . . it was as if a photograph had suddenly come to life and began to talk, smile, nod its head, and look this way and that.[13]

Between AT&T, RCA, and other companies, as well as independent inventors like Farnsworth, a lot of competition then existed among TV inventors and developers. Some were more technically advanced than others. Also, each had an individual approach to solving technical problems and presenting the new technology to the public.

These competing ideas and arguments eventually came before the Federal Communications Commission (FCC). Congress created that organization in 1934 to regulate communications systems in the United States, including radio, the telegraph, telephones, and the emerging medium of television. RCA and others were already beginning to talk about introducing a commercial version of TV marketed to the public. But the FCC decided that before that could happen television developers needed to achieve certain standards of quality. "Television is not yet ready for public service on a national scale," an FCC spokesman said in 1938. "There does not appear to be any immediate outlook for the recognition of television service on a commercial

The Powers of the FCC

The Federal Communications Commission (FCC) was created by the U.S. Congress in 1934. Its functions are to make and enforce rules relating to the broadcasting industry, including issuing licenses to radio and television stations. A station that breaks an FCC rule can be punished. First, it receives a warning letter. If the station continues to violate the rule, the FCC can force it to pay a fine. If that does not solve the dispute, FCC officials can meet to consider whether the station's license should be renewed. (Without an FCC license, the station cannot continue to do business.) The FCC officials who make such decisions are five in number. They are appointed by the president of the United States and are approved by the U.S. Senate. Each commissioner serves a five-year term.

basis."[14] This somewhat guarded attitude toward television would soon change, however.

NBC Takes the Lead

The single most important force in pushing for a commercial, publicly marketed TV industry in the 1930s was RCA, still headed by David Sarnoff. Although Farnsworth had earlier won the patent suit that RCA had brought against him, the persistent Sarnoff remained undaunted. He simply did an end run around this setback by paying Farnsworth a licensing fee (or royalty) for use of his ideas. Sarnoff then proceeded to combine Farnsworth's and Zworykin's technical advances and assigned RCA's TV development activities to the company's radio division, the National Broadcasting Company (NBC), which had formed in 1926.

These moves were only part of a larger, very bold plan Sarnoff had developed for making television broadcasting a big business. First, he planned to build the first modern television transmission station, preferably not far from RCA's research labs in New York City. Second, Sarnoff intended to manufacture hundreds of experimental TV sets and place them at strategic spots in the region; these would be used to test the system and begin building public interest. Finally, Sarnoff said he wanted to "develop an experimental program service with the necessary studio technique to determine the most acceptable form of television programs."[15] Thus, Sarnoff had wisely set out to master and dominate the three central pillars of any viable television industry: broadcasting stations, TV sets to receive the broadcasts, and programs to show on the TV sets.

NBC's first major broadcast, shown here, was of the 1939 World's Fair in New York City.

To kick off the implementation of his grand scheme, Sarnoff shrewdly took advantage of the fact that the next World's Fair was scheduled to occur in New York City in the spring of 1939. First, he ordered several dozen small TV sets to be placed on the fairgrounds, at RCA's headquarters, and in selected homes in the general area. A camera at the fairgrounds was hooked up to a transmitter in a nearby bus. Its job was to relay the TV signal to a tower atop the Empire State Building, 8 miles (13km) away. From there, the signal would transmit to the various TV sets. On the demonstration's scheduled day, April 20, 1939, the camera took shots of the fair's major structures, then focused on NBC president Lenox R. Lohr. Lohr introduced Sarnoff, who told his small audience:

Now we add radio sight to sound. It is with a feeling of humbleness that I come to this moment of announcing the birth in this country of a new art so important in its implications that it is bound to affect all society. It is an art which shines like a torch of hope in a troubled world.[16]

Sarnoff realized that to attract a TV-viewing audience he had to present more than some men standing at a lectern and talking. So he initiated the first American night of television programming a couple of weeks later, on May 3. Noted bandleader Fred Waring appeared with his musicians, and the famous film animator Walt Disney introduced a new character, Donald Duck's cousin, Gus.

NBC also presented the first news broadcast, hosted by acclaimed journalist Lowell Thomas. In addition, NBC soon began regular programming on Wednesday and Friday evenings from 8:00 to 9:00 P.M.

These broadcasts created a lot of "buzz" (entertainment lingo for interest) among both broadcasters and average people. Indeed, many people in the New York area were eager to buy TV sets. However, their interest in the new electronic medium did not overcome the then-major expense of these sets. RCA's set with a 5-inch (13-cm) screen retailed for about $200; its 12-inch (30-cm) set cost $600. At the time, the average American family made about $1,850 a year, so the vast majority of people could not afford to buy a TV. As a result, RCA sold only three thousand sets in 1939. Sarnoff, who had anticipated selling as many as one hundred thousand sets the first year, was sorely disappointed.

In fact, Sarnoff and other TV pioneers faced a dilemma that was circular in nature. As an October 1939 article in the journal *Public Opinion Quarterly* described it:

The costs of sponsoring television programs are ten to fifteen times as great as radio. . . . If such entertainment is not forthcoming, [TV] sets will not be sold. If sets are not sold, businesses will not advertise via television. If business does not advertise, programs comparable to radio's will not be forthcoming. A way to break that [vicious] circle must be found.[17]

The Formation of TV Networks

Sarnoff hoped to overcome these marketing difficulties. However, he encountered two obstacles. One was that it was hard for TV to compete with radio. Radio programs were well established and popular, and radio sets were fairly inexpensive. By 1940 there were some 50 million radios in the United States, and about 80 percent of the country's households had at least one radio. Even more daunting for Sarnoff and RCA: In 1939 World War II erupted in Europe; the United States entered the conflict in 1941. Television development came to a virtual halt during the war as researchers at RCA and other electronics companies spent most

After World War II four TV networks emerged: NBC, CBS, ABC, and the DuMont Network.

of their time working on military projects. (Sarnoff went to Europe and helped to restore France's radio industry, which the Germans had largely destroyed. He was awarded a brigadier general's star and thereafter went by the title "General Sarnoff.")

When the war ended in 1945, RCA and other companies were eager to resume the development of commercial television. At this point there were three competing radio networks (organizations each having multiple stations). In addition to NBC, there was the Columbia Broadcasting System (CBS), which had formed in 1927. There was also the American Broadcasting Corporation (ABC), which emerged in 1943. A fourth network, devoted to TV only, the DuMont Network (named for its founder, American engineer Allen DuMont), appeared in 1947.

One major reason for the rise of TV networks was that, during television's early days, radio waves could carry television signals only limited distances. So any one station or channel could reach only a local audience and was unable to distribute its programs to a national audience. However, if many stations spread across the country formed an alliance, or network, they could all carry the programming of a single producer, such as NBC. Hillstrom lists some other reasons why forming TV networks made sense at the time:

> Another advantage of the network arrangement is that it spreads the cost of creating programs over a large number of affiliated [allied or associated] stations. It is significantly cheaper to produce one program and distribute it to many local stations than for every local station to produce its own programs. Networks also help advertisers to reach larger audiences by placing commercials on national broadcasts rather than local programs.[18]

Thus, in 1947, four TV networks were poised on the brink of exploiting the potential of commercial television. No one, including the executives at the networks, realized at the time just how fast the new medium would grow, or how truly enormous the TV-viewing audience would become. The modern television era, which would change America and eventually the world forever, was about to begin.

Chapter Two

Building a National Audience

In the late 1940s, with television still an emerging, untested industry, the infant TV networks concentrated on attracting new viewers and building a national audience. The key to the success of this effort, of course, was showing programs that would appeal to as many viewers as possible. To this end, in June 1946 NBC broadcast the heavyweight title boxing match between Joe Louis and Billy Conn, staged at Yankee Stadium in New York City. About 140,000 people in four cities (New York City; Philadelphia; Schenectady, New York; and Washington, D.C.) watched the fight. Not all of them had their own TV sets. Typically, dozens or more viewers would gather around a neighbor's set; also, to drum up business, many stores that sold TVs allowed the public to come in and watch for free. The number of viewers who saw the broadcast was then seen as huge, prompting a Philadelphia newspaper to report, "The winner—Television!"[19]

NBC scored an even bigger success by televising baseball's World Series in September and October 1947, again in a four-city broadcast. An estimated 3.8 million people watched the games. And stores reported a sharp spike in TV-set sales in October and November. NBC also pioneered the first hour-long weekly program in 1946. Titled *Hour Glass,* it was a variety show featuring comedy acts, dancing, and musical numbers. In addition, NBC's weekly dramatic series, *Kraft Television Theater,* began a successful eleven-year run in 1947.

The number of people who watched these weekly programs were very few by today's standards. Only about 44,000 TV sets existed in American homes by the end of 1947 (compared with more than 100 million today). TV producers and programmers determined that most of the owners of these sets fit a certain profile. As one expert observer put it:

Pioneering TV set owners lived principally in cities or suburbs, were more likely to buy [a set] if neither very rich nor very poor, were relatively well-educated, young, had two or three children in the household, and were quick to praise the new technology.[20]

It became increasingly clear to network executives that attracting more viewers like these would require both more hours of programming each day and more appealing programming.

"Mr. Television"

TV programmers tried just about every entertainment and informational format they could think of in the early days of TV. In addition to boxing, baseball, and other sports shows, they aired news reports, dramas, and situation comedies (later called sitcoms for short). Many of the early sitcoms were based on successful radio shows. Among these were *The Goldbergs* (about a Jewish family in New York City), which premiered on TV in 1949; also in 1949, *Life of Riley* (about a bungling but big-hearted factory worker and his family); and in 1951, *Amos 'n' Andy* (about two black men who run a taxi cab company in Chicago).

These shows attracted what the networks viewed as decent-sized audiences. But the most successful format by far during that era was the comedy-variety series pioneered by Milton Berle, who became TV's first superstar. Berle was a nightclub entertainer who had gotten his start in vaudeville. (Vaudeville consisted of stage shows highly popular in America from the 1880s to 1940s; they pre-

sented variety acts, including singers, dancers, comedians, magicians, acrobats, and trained animals.) The famous American comedian Bob Hope once quipped, "When vaudeville died, television was the box they put it in."[21]

Berle made these words ring true. Beginning in March 1948 he hosted NBC's *Texaco Star Theater,* a nonstop array of outlandish costumes, hokey jokes, energetic musical numbers, and animal acts. Berle was able to convince many famous film and nightclub stars to be guests on the show, among them Frank Sinatra, Ethel Merman, and Pearl Bailey. This gave the program some strong star power, but home audiences especially loved Berle's outrageous comic routines. "He was a bug-eyed mass of nervous energy onscreen," Edgerton writes, "flicking his left eyelid from time to time with his right pinky finger, whistling through his teeth, and even slapping his hands together in a kind of do-it-yourself rim shot after a series of well-worn jokes crested like a wave over the crowd in front of him."[22] Noted TV critic Richard Corliss later added, "If it were possible, [Berle] would have stuck his head through the TV screen [and] licked your face."[23]

Berle's antics, aired on Tuesday nights at 8:00 P.M., drew an amazing 75 percent of the entire existing TV audience, about 5 million people. The *New Yorker* exclaimed that his show had launched "a phenomenon of massive proportions."[24] That phenomenon included enticing many more Americans to buy TV sets. By early 1950, 9 percent of the nation's

Milton Berle and Ethel Merman perform on the incredibly successful Texaco Star Theater.

households—encompassing an estimated 3,875,000 people—had TVs. It is no wonder that Berle became widely known as "Mr. Television."

Berle's success, along with that of other early TV stars, had another far-reaching effect. It induced many sponsors of radio programs to switch their allegiance to TV. National sponsors left radio for TV at record rates, moving the show-business trade magazine *Variety* to describe the exodus as "the greatest exhibition of mass hysteria in [show]biz annals."[25]

Other Variety Hits

Several other variety shows built on the success of Berle and his Texaco show. In fact, vaudeville-style programs made up fully one-third of TV programming in 1951. Many of these shows featured, either as hosts or guests, many comedians who had attained success in vaudeville, radio, and/or films. Among them were Jack Benny, Bob Hope, Ed Wynn, Groucho Marx, George Burns and his wife Gracie Allen, and the great Jimmy Durante, known for his gravel voice and oversized nose.

Among the most successful of these shows was *Toast of the Town,* which premiered in June 1948 on the CBS network. CBS chief William S. Paley hired *New York Daily News* columnist Ed Sullivan to host the show. Most people at first thought this was an odd choice since Sullivan was not a performer and had a stiff,

Ed Sullivan, center, with musical guests the Beatles. The Ed Sullivan Show *was a huge hit.*

awkward on-camera presence. But as Paley later recalled, Sullivan "knew the world of entertainment and he promised that he could produce a good show cheaply."[26] Sullivan made good on this promise. Beginning with the comedy team of Dean Martin and Jerry Lewis, he presented a seemingly never-ending array of top show-business talent. The program, renamed *The Ed Sullivan Show* in 1955, became a huge hit and lasted twenty-three years. (In the early 1960s, Sullivan made history by booking the Beatles in their American TV premiere.)

Equally popular was *The Red Skelton Show,* which debuted in September 1951. The son of a circus clown, Skelton made his name in vaudeville during the 1930s and radio during the early 1940s. His TV variety show, which lasted for twenty-one years, featured guest singers and comedians. But the highlight each week was when Skelton performed one or more of the stock characters he had created over the years. Two of the more popular were the country bumpkin Clem Kaddiddlehopper and the mild-mannered hobo Freddie the Freeloader.

Another groundbreaking variety program was *Your Show of Shows*, which ran from 1950 to 1954. The program was unusual in several ways. Perhaps most unusual was the fact that it was the joint presentation of two networks, NBC and DuMont. (The year after the show's run ended, DuMont, unable to compete with the other three networks, went out of business.) Another factor that made *Your Show of Shows* unique was that it ran for ninety, rather than sixty, minutes. Finally, its format revolved less around old-style vaudeville gags and more around humorous parodies (takeoffs) of various aspects of modern life; in this respect, its repertory company of talented comedians, including Sid Caesar, Imogene Coca, and Carl Reiner, was the direct forerunner of the casts of *Saturday Night Live.*

The Success of Middle-Class Sitcoms

Variety shows did not remain number one in viewer popularity for long, however. The sitcom quickly gained this position, in large part because of the success of a single show—*I Love Lucy.* Lucille Ball had been a moderately successful film actress during the 1930s and 1940s and had also done some radio. But in *I Love Lucy,* which ran from 1951 to 1957, she finally hit her stride. She portrayed housewife Lucy Ricardo, who was married to Cuban bandleader Ricky Ricardo, played by her real-life husband Desi Arnaz (who actually *was* a Cuban bandleader). Lucy's relentless attempts to better her life, often by trying to break into show business, invariably got her into trouble, with wacky, humorous results.

Part of the show's incredible success derived from the fact that many Americans could relate to Lucy. In an over-the-top, comical way, her situation mirrored many aspects of their own lives. "Lucy and Ricky Ricardo prospered in the pattern followed by others in postwar America," modern biographer Kathleen Brady explains. "The young city couple grew in affluence, bought a television set and washing machine, had a baby, ventured across the country . . . and ultimately moved to the suburbs."[27]

In retrospect, it is clear that *I Love Lucy* was also an important transitional show from earlier sitcoms to a newer batch that aired during the late 1950s and early 1960s. The tastes of the TV audience were changing by the mid-1950s, in part because it was bigger and more diverse. No longer concentrated mainly in the northeastern sector of the country, that audience consisted of people spread across the entire nation, including the American heartland. As a result, there was more interest among viewers for comedies that better reflected their own situations. *The Goldbergs, Life of Riley,* and comic genius Jackie Gleason's *The Honeymooners* (1955–1956) had depicted the lives of lower-class blue-collar workers. But large parts of America were increasingly concentrated in suburbia and dominated by middle-class, white-collar workers (who were also mostly racially white). Edgerton points out that *I Love Lucy* provided a link "between the urban, ethnic, working-class sitcoms of the late 1940s and early 1950s [and] the increasingly [middle-class] domestic comedies"[28] of the late 1950s.

One of the first successful sitcoms to reflect this new cultural dynamic was *Father Knows Best* (1954–1963). It starred former film actor Robert Young as the head of the suburban Anderson family, which featured three school-age children (two girls and a boy) and a comfortable, middle-class home. *Leave It to Beaver* (1957–1963) had a

Desilu: Pioneer of the Sitcom

Lucille Ball's personal production company, Desilu (*Desi* for her husband, Desi Arnaz, and *lu* for Lucy), pioneered numerous shooting techniques used later by hundreds of TV sitcoms. The members of the Desilu team converted a Los Angeles TV studio, adding bleachers for three hundred spectators so that they could film before a live audience. Also, Oscar-winning camera operator Karl Freund, whom Lucy knew from her movie days at MGM, designed a special, all-purpose lighting setup. It allowed the show to be shot without the frequent, time-consuming lighting changes that are routine on movie sets. Desilu also introduced a multiple camera setup, allowing the action to be recorded from several angles at the same time; the footage from the separate cameras was later edited to tell the comic story in a smooth, fast-paced manner. By the end of the 1950s, Desilu had grown so much in size and influence that it was nearly as large as major film studios like MGM and Twentieth Century Fox.

Many Americans felt they could relate to Lucy (Lucille Ball, left) on the I Love Lucy *show.*

similar format, only with two young boys. Such shows presented an idealized, in some ways sanitized, view of American life that conveniently ignored various ongoing societal problems, including the struggle of American blacks for equality. Today, in reruns, they appeal to some people who nostalgically long for what they mistakenly see as simpler, kinder, happier times.

The Rise of the TV Western

Thanks in part to popular sitcoms like *Lucy*, increasing numbers of Americans bought TV sets during the 1950s. In 1951 about 22 percent of homes in the country had sets; by 1960 that number had grown to an impressive 87 percent. The number of television stations broadcasting network shows also grew enormously, from 107 in 1951 to about 500 in 1960.

The Fairness Doctrine

As commercial television grew in size and influence in the 1950s, the FCC wanted to make sure that that industry did not abuse its increasing power and that it served the public interest. In particular, the FCC felt it was important that no single point of view on a controversial issue be allowed to dominate and overshadow all others. In 1959, at the urging of the FCC, Congress introduced the Fairness Doctrine. This rule required that broadcasters reserve a set amount of air time for issues of public importance. It also called for giving equal time to both sides of an argument. That way, the viewers could hear both sides and form their own opinions in an informed way. The Fairness Doctrine worked well for several decades, but it was eliminated in 1987 as part of an effort to make the broadcast industry less regulated and thereby freer to make its own decisions. Since that time, critics say, many TV news organizations have become more biased in their coverage of controversial issues.

This increase in TV's penetration into American homes and society was also due to the popularity of the Western genre on television. Depicting various aspects of America's rustic, often violent "cowboy" or "Old West" culture of the middle to late 1800s, sixteen Western shows were on the air by 1957. By 1960, at the height of the genre's success, there were twenty-eight TV Westerns.

Cowboy shows, including *The Lone Ranger* and *The Roy Rogers Show,* had been popular on radio. The public had also long enjoyed movie Westerns such as *Stagecoach* (1939), with John Wayne. But the genre struck a new and deep chord with TV audiences. "Westerns held appeal for TV viewers," Laurie C. Hillstrom suggests, "because they emphasized traditional American values and offered a clear contrast between the good guys and the bad guys."[29]

A prime example of the early TV Westerns that routinely exploited these themes was CBS's *Gunsmoke.* One of the longest-running television series ever, it aired from 1955 to 1975 and was rated the number one show on TV for four years in a row (1957–1961). Tall, lanky James Arness played Matt Dillon, sheriff of Dodge City, Kansas, where lawbreakers regularly threatened the town and its citizens. Another stalwart lawman was the subject of ABC's hit *The Life and Legend of Wyatt Earp* (1955–1961). Other popular Westerns included *Wagon Train* (1957–1962), *Maverick* (1957–1962), *The Rifleman* (1958–1963), *Rawhide* (1959–1966), and *Bonanza* (1959–1973). *Rawhide* benefited from the sex appeal of the

Pictured here is the cast of the Western **Gunsmoke**, *which ran for twenty years.*

hunky young Clint Eastwood. Much of the appeal of *The Rifleman* (with Chuck Connors in the title role) and *Bonanza* (with Lorne Greene as the head of the Cartwright clan) came from their depiction of close-knit families struggling to create prosperous, peaceful lives in a society fraught with uncertainty and danger.

One of the most original and offbeat of the TV Westerns of that era was *Have Gun—Will Travel*. On the air from 1957 to 1963, it was almost always rated in the top four television shows. Film actor Richard Boone played Paladin, portrayed as a sort of medieval knight transplanted into nineteenth-century America. A scholar, opera buff, authority on world history, and wine expert who also spoke numerous languages, Paladin was in addition a professional gunfighter whose speed on the draw was unsurpassed in the American West. Show-business historian David Rothel sums up the show's unique format:

> Set in the period following the Civil War, the episodes usually began in the Sumptuous Hotel Carlton in San Francisco, where [the] sophisticated [Paladin] resided in a suite. . . . The daily newspaper [alerted him to] a problem where his assistance could be useful, or [someone] would request Paladin's assistance to resolve a matter in some distant western town. . . . Whatever the manner of contact, Paladin usually found need to flash his business card ("Have gun will travel. Wire Paladin, San Francisco.") And then, dressed in

his black "business" outfit, [he] was on the trail to trouble.[30]

Although a few TV Westerns continued into the late 1960s and beyond, the genre as a whole lost steam during the early to middle 1960s. One reason may be that there were so many cowboy shows that the public grew tired of them. Some television critics suggest that, in addition, new social movements, including those involving civil rights and women's rights, made Westerns seem too simplistic and old-fashioned.

Adventures in Daytime TV

Whatever the reasons for the decline of the TV Western, other television genres that had begun in the 1950s retained their popularity or even increased their audiences. This was particularly true in the area of daytime shows (as opposed to "prime-time" shows, which ran from 8:00 to 11:00 P.M.). Some of the earliest daytime programs were children's shows. Several were half-hour adventures with either human heroes (as in *The Lone Ranger*, about a masked, crime-fighting former Texas Ranger) or animal heroes (as in *Lassie*, about a faithful collie dog who repeatedly saves her master from harm).

Some children's shows gained huge, loyal audiences and had very long runs on television. *Howdy Doody* was one. Airing from 1947 to 1960, it featured human host Buffalo Bob Smith and his freckle-faced puppet friend Howdy Doody. There were loads of jokes, silly skits, and songs, usually witnessed by a live studio audience of children (the "peanut gallery"). Another

Children's shows such as Howdy Doody *often had long runs on television.*

children's hit was *Captain Kangaroo,* which debuted in 1955 and ran for thirty-six years. The title character, played by Bob Keeshan, entertained youngsters while ensuring that each show had a positive educational message. In addition, Walt Disney created several widely popular shows during the 1950s and 1960s, including *Disneyland* (later renamed *Walt Disney's Wonderful World of Color*) and *The Mickey Mouse Club.*

Meanwhile, television programmers were adapting to women's daytime routines to better exploit the growing daytime audience. These shows "could be watched in a distracted manner," Edgerton points out. "Women could adjust their housekeeping routines [by] turning the volume up [and] performing chores such as ironing and mending within earshot . . . of the TV set."[31]

In particular, housewives and other people home a lot in the daytime became hooked on serial dramas, which came to be called soap operas. This name derived from the fact that the early versions were sponsored largely by companies that sold laundry detergent. These shows featured long, complex stories lasting months or even years and numerous characters, usually citizens of fictional American towns (such as Pine Valley, Pennsylvania, in *All My Children*). The first TV soap was DuMont's *Faraway Hill,* which premiered in 1946. Another soap, *The Guiding Light,* had started as an NBC radio show in 1937; CBS brought it to TV in 1952, and it aired its fifteen thousandth episode in September 2006, making it the longest-running TV drama ever. Other popular early soaps included *General*

The Success of the Disney Brand

All experts agree that animator and filmmaker Walt Disney was one of the giants of the television medium. Beginning in the early 1950s, there has never been a year when TV did not carry some kind of Disney program. Generations of children have grown up enjoying *Walt Disney's Wonderful World of Color, The Mickey Mouse Club, Zorro,* and the diverse offerings of the Disney Channel on cable. On television, as in the movies, Disney's brand name became associated with fun, make-believe, and high-quality family entertainment. His first TV show, called *Disneyland* after his renowned California theme park, began on the ABC network in October 1954. To both Disney's and ABC's delight, it was an immediate hit. In fact, many people rushed out and bought TV sets for the first time just so they could see Disney films in their own homes. Also, trying to cash in on the Disney TV craze, dozens of new TV stations opened around the country and signed on with ABC.

Hospital (debuted in 1963), *One Life to Live* (1968), and *All My Children* (1970).

Housewives and other daytime viewers were also drawn to talk shows and game shows. Between 1949 and 1973 about half of all daytime programming consisted of talk shows. Most were modeled on the first successful one, NBC's *Today,* hosted by Dave Garroway, who engaged in mild-mannered chat with entertainers and others. Host Phil Donahue took the format a step further in the 1970s by inviting more controversial guests and exploring edgier topics.

In a lighter vein, most of the game shows of the 1950s and 1960s involved ordinary people playing the games to win prizes. One of the first and most successful entries in this genre was *The Price Is Right,* which began in 1956 and is still on the air. A more intellectual daytime game show, *Jeopardy!* (created by Merv Griffin), debuted in 1964 and also remains popular today.

Overall, TV came to provide a regular form of escape for daytime viewers during the 1950s and 1960s. The television networks wanted to do the same for a much larger audience during prime time by making the vast majority of Americans habitual TV watchers. And during the 1960s and 1970s, they succeeded beyond their wildest dreams.

Chapter Three

TV Becomes a Great Escape

During the 1960s and 1970s, network executives naturally wanted to continue the great expansion of the TV audience that had begun during the 1950s. They wanted to sell more TV sets. They also wanted to entice those who owned sets to spend more hours of each day watching the programs the networks provided since that would bring in more revenue for both the sponsors and the networks.

The central question was: What kinds of programs would attract the most viewers? The network chiefs were well aware that the country and the world were very different in the 1960s than they had been in the 1950s. The civil rights movement increased in intensity and inspired violence, including the assassination of its leading figure, Martin Luther King Jr.; the Cold War between the United States and the Soviet Union intensified and seemed to heighten the risk of nuclear war; and the United States became involved in a disastrous war in Vietnam, which seriously polarized the country into prowar and antiwar camps. The networks did cover these controversial topics in their news broadcasts, but they worried that dealing with them in their dramas, comedies, and other shows might offend and turn off viewers. So they chose instead, at least at first, to produce a great deal of escapist fare, including many goofy comedies.

This period also witnessed two major developments in television. One was the spread of television technology and programming across most of the globe. Although TVs and TV programming existed in England, France, Germany, and several other nations in the late 1940s and 1950s, large-scale television industries like the one in the United States did not develop in most of these countries until the 1960s. Moreover, it was not until the late 1960s, and in some cases well into the

1970s, that TV programming of any kind reached many of the poorer third world nations.

The Coming of Color

The other pivotal TV development in the period was the swift and large-scale changeover from black-and-white sets to color ones. Various forms of color TV existed well before commercial television began to take off in the late 1940s. In fact, in Scotland John L. Baird, one of the pioneers of mechanical TV, built a mechanical color system as early as 1928. Soon afterward, in America, Bell Laboratories produced a color mechanical TV image on a screen the size of a postage stamp. However, the color generated by these devices was not very realistic, and the systems themselves were primitive by later standards.

The first major breakthrough in color television was the work of CBS engineer Peter Goldmark. In March 1940 he went to see the Hollywood blockbuster *Gone with the Wind.* "For me it was a uniquely exhilarating [exciting] experience," he later recalled,

> not because of the performances or the story, but because it was the first color movie I had seen, and the color was magnificent. I could hardly think of going back to the phosphor images of regular black-and-white television. All through the long, four-hour movie I was obsessed with the thought of applying color to television.[32]

A test audience views CBS's demonstration of color television.

How Electronic Color TV Works

The electronic color television system perfected in the 1950s and 1960s works somewhat differently than the black-and-white version of electronic TV. In the latter, a single beam of electrons passes through the cathode-ray tube and strikes the back of the screen. In the color version, by contrast, three such beams move through the tube and strike the screen. One beam is red, one is green, and one is blue. The screen of a color set has thousands of tiny red, green, and blue dots (called phosphors). When the three colored beams touch these dots, they glow. The red ones glow if activated by redness in the red beam, the green ones glow when excited by greenness in the green beam, and so forth. In this way, the three beams in a sense paint a color picture on the dot-covered screen.

In the months that followed, Goldmark developed a color system that utilized wheels to which he attached red, blue, and green filters. One wheel spun behind the lens of a TV camera; the other spun in front of the cathode-ray tube inside a TV set. This system combined various elements of mechanical TV and electronic TV. Goldmark demonstrated the system to members of the FCC, hoping they would approve it as the industry standard. Though they were impressed, they felt that more work was needed before they could take that step. Soon afterward the United States entered World War II, forcing Goldmark and other CBS engineers to postpone most of their television research.

After the war, Goldmark resumed his color TV research. Over at RCA, David Sarnoff became worried that, if the FCC approved CBS's color system, both RCA

and NBC would lose a lot of money. It "would set back the cause of our technology by a generation," he remarked. "RCA will never allow this counterfeit scheme to be foisted on the American people,"[33] he added. One argument Sarnoff offered the FCC was that Goldmark's system was partly mechanical and that the FCC had long before made electronic TV the industry standard. As a result, the FCC again ruled against approving the CBS color system. Meanwhile, RCA began developing its own color TV technology.

Not to be outdone, in 1949 Goldmark boldly demonstrated his system to a test audience. Its members were impressed, which created some modest demand for color TV; so the following year the FCC relented and approved the CBS system. However, the marketplace quickly reversed the effects of this victory. By mid-

1951 only about twenty-five color sets had been bought by American consumers, and CBS executives decided that this tiny audience did not justify proceeding with color broadcasts, which were then quite expensive.

The failure of CBS's color system opened the way for RCA. In 1953 the latter developed an all-electronic color system and the following year began selling color TVs to the public. Sales were slow at first. This was partly because color sets were much more expensive than black-and-white ones; an RCA color set then cost one thousand dollars, the same amount as a new car. Also, early color sets had smaller screens than most black-and-white sets. A major boost came in 1960–1961, when NBC began broadcasting Walt Disney's show *Disneyland* in color. This prompted large numbers of viewers to buy color sets, which by that time had come down in price. Color TVs sold briskly during the 1960s. By 1972 more than half of all the homes in the United States had color sets.

Escapist Sitcoms

The addition of color helped to expand the size of the American TV audience. In 1960, 45,750,000 TV sets existed in the United States, of which only a few thousand were

Color TV sets sold quickly in the 1960s as they became more reasonably priced.

The Marriage of TV and Sports

Some experts contend that television and professional sports were made for each other. And since the early days of TV, they have entered into a sort of marriage that has greatly benefited both in various ways. Early television fans were thrilled that watching their screens seemed to put them in the middle of the action, and many became enthusiastic, loyal sports fans. The sports teams also benefited when TV introduced several lesser-known sports, including tennis, golf, hockey, and auto racing, to a large American viewing audience. In addition, over time TV exposure made many sports teams wealthy. (In 2005, the National Football League earned $3.7 billion from its TV contracts.) Likewise, some of the athletes involved became national celebrities. Television coverage also changed the operations of several major sports leagues. The National Hockey League, for example, expanded from six to thirty teams in order to reach more of the lucrative TV markets. On the flip side, the television industry benefited hugely from sports. The desire to see broadcasts of championship boxing matches and the yearly Army-Navy football games boosted the sales of TV sets during the late 1940s. In addition, broadcasts of football's Super Bowl and the Olympic Games over the years have significantly expanded TV audiences and ratings.

color TVs. By 1972 U.S. TVs numbered 62,350,000, of which 32,800,000 (53 percent of the total) were color sets. At the same time, color was one factor that enticed many existing TV viewers to watch their sets more often than before. Average American viewers watched four to five hours of TV per day in 1960; that number had increased to more than six hours per day by 1975.

The more television that people watched, the more the programs became a fixed part of their daily schedules and, in general, their lives. These programs also became a welcome means of escape from personal problems as well as from what many viewed as too much unset-tling news about an increasingly troubled world.

Nowhere was this public desire to be distracted more evident than in the tremendous success of CBS's sitcom *The Beverly Hillbillies* (1962–1971). One of the most popular shows of the 1960s, it became the top-rated TV program three weeks after its premiere and stayed in that coveted spot for the next two years; during that period an estimated 60 million people tuned in to the show each week. It showcased the goofy antics of the Clampetts, a poor backwoods family that suddenly strikes it rich and moves into a mansion in Beverly Hills, California. In a humorous manner, Laurie C. Hillstrom explains, "Each episode contrast[ed] the Clampett family's rural values with the shallow materialism of their wealthy neighbors."[34] Most critics called the show frivolous, or at best silly, but viewers found it ideal escapist fare.

Moreover, *Hillbillies* served as a model for dozens of other lightweight sitcoms that exploited the "fish-out-of-water" theme (in which the main character or characters find themselves in unfamiliar or strange surroundings). *Green Acres* (1965–1971), for instance, reversed the Clampetts's situation. A New York lawyer, played by Eddie Albert, leaves his comfortable life in the big city and becomes a farmer in a rural community inhabited by country bumpkins. Similarly, in *Gilligan's Island* (1964–1967) a group of tourists are marooned on a desert island lacking modern conveniences; in *My Favorite Martian* (1963–1966), an alien being must cope with human foibles after he is marooned on Earth; and a witch (*Bewitched*, 1964–1972), a genie (*I Dream of Jeannie*, 1965–1970), and a family of movie-style monsters (*The Munsters*, 1964–1966) find themselves oddballs in a world of "normal" folk. No less silly, nor less funny, was the talking horse on *Mr. Ed* (1961–1965) and the bumbling James Bond–wannabe Maxwell Smart (played by Don Adams) in the spy spoof *Get Smart* (1965–1970).

A few more conventional, realistic TV sitcoms also became popular in the 1960s. Chief among them were *The Dick Van Dyke Show* (1961–1966) and *The Andy Griffith Show* (1960–1968). Their settings contrasted sharply, as Van Dyke's stories unfolded in the suburbs of New York City and Griffith's took place in a small, rural North Carolina town. However, they had much in common. Each featured a family with a hardworking, appealing father figure. And each dealt with common home and workplace situations in a lighthearted manner. Moreover, though realistic on the surface, these shows remained firmly escapist in content and approach. "Both avoided controversial topics," University of Tennessee scholar Barbara Moore points out, "and radiated with a humanity that made viewers feel good about the world."[35]

The comedy TV series Get Smart *starred Barbara Feldon as Agent 99 and Don Adams as the bumbling Maxwell Smart.*

Increasingly Realistic Comedies

This tendency for TV shows to ignore rapidly changing social situations and values could not continue indefinitely, however. The late 1960s and much of the 1970s witnessed widespread social turmoil and change that reached into homes, workplaces, schools, and most other societal settings. The civil rights movement, in which blacks and other minorities demanded equal treatment and respect, increased in scope; and women fought for greater social independence, respect, and equal pay with men. In addition, large sectors of the public became disillusioned with the government and other aspects of the sociopolitical "establishment." In part this was a result of the rising death toll in the increasingly unpopular Vietnam War as well as the spectacle of U.S. president Richard Nixon caught in illegal activities and forced to resign his high office.

Despite the seriousness of these trends and events, American TV audiences still wanted to watch sitcoms. But increasingly they turned away from more frivolous formats and embraced ones that better reflected what was happening in the nation and the world. As Hillstrom puts it, "The most popular and influential shows of the 1970s tended to present more realistic pictures of American working people and families. Many of them also featured a darker brand of humor that seemed to fit the troubled times."[36] These programs highlighted not only the struggles of average Americans but also dealt with dysfunctional characters and situations as well as some of the common fears and prejudices of the day.

One of the most visible and controversial examples of this new trend was *All in the Family*, which ran from 1971 to 1983. It showcased the dysfunctional Bunker family, including the father, Archie (played by Carroll O'Connor), a right-wing conservative and proud bigot who called his wife (Jean Stapleton) a "dingbat" and son-in-law (Rob Reiner) "meathead." "The program traded in racism and stereotypes," Moore writes, along with "taboo subjects such as impotency and miscarriage and anything else that could be branded controversial, including the unheard-of-to-that-time sound of a toilet flushing."[37]

Archie Bunker and his family dealt frequently with prejudice and other racial and ethnic issues, as did a number of new shows built around black, Hispanic, and other minority characters and families. *Sanford and Son* (1972–1977), for example, portrayed an African American man and his son struggling to survive on the edge of urban poverty. *Good Times* (1974–1979) and *The Jeffersons* (1975–1985) also showed the lives of black families. And *Welcome Back, Kotter* (1975–1979), set in a high school in Brooklyn, New York, presented a racial and ethnic cross-section of society, including young Italian Americans, African Americans, and a Puerto Rican Jew.

Commentary about social and political issues was also prominent in sitcoms dealing with women and war. For the first time in TV history, independent women with professional aspirations and strong personal agendas became the lead char-

Shows like The Jeffersons, *starring Isabel Sanford and Sherman Hemsley, addressed racial issues in society.*

acters of recurring series. The most successful entry in this genre was *The Mary Tyler Moore Show* (1970–1977). It inspired women across the nation to seek careers and be more assertive in dealing with others. Meanwhile, many viewers with both prowar and antiwar sentiments tuned in habitually to CBS's huge hit *M*A*S*H* (1972–1983). Although the show chronicled the exploits of medical personnel in the Korean War of the early 1950s, 1970s audiences saw strong parallels with the Vietnam conflict. *M*A*S*H* was so popular that its final show drew the largest audience for a single TV episode in history, some 125 million viewers!

A Wide Range of Dramas

Like the comedies of the 1960s, most of the dramatic shows of that decade fell into the escapist category. The intent of the producers of these programs was to entertain viewers by transporting them into specific and hopefully interesting societal niches, such as the courtroom, the police station, and the hospital. A majority of the TV dramas of the 1970s followed the same pattern. With a few exceptions, these shows lacked the cutting-edge commentary about social, political, racial, and ethnic problems so often explored in the sitcoms of the 1970s. (Still, some of these dramas did break some ground in racial and ethnic matters by including blacks and Hispanics as regular recurring characters. For example, both the detective drama *Mannix* [1967–1975] and the spy thriller *Mission: Impossible* [1966–1973] featured black performers in key roles.)

One of the longest-running and most popular dramas of the era was the courtroom series *Perry Mason,* which enjoyed a 245-episode run from 1957 until 1966. Based on the best-selling detective novels of Erle Stanley Gardner, the show starred veteran film actor Raymond Burr as a defense attorney who seemingly never lost a case. Moore recalls the formula followed in nearly every episode:

> In the first half of the program the crime in question and Mason's client would be introduced, and the client would be wrongly charged with the crime. During the second half, a detailed investigation, preliminary hearing, or trial would be held and Mason would, invariably, clear his client and expose the guilt of the real criminal, who would promptly break down and confess on the spot.[38]

The other dramas that drew large audiences covered a wide range of settings and genres. Medical shows were highly popular, especially *Dr. Kildare* (1961–1966), starring Richard Chamberlain, and *Ben Casey* (1961–1966), with Vince Edwards. Family dramas also did well. Among the highest-rated entries in this category were *The Waltons* (1972–1981) and *Little House on the Prairie* (1974–1983). These and several similar shows chronicled the daily lives of large families eking out livings in frontier or rural settings. As might be expected in an era of escapist entertainment, science fiction was also a big audience draw. Particularly popular or noteworthy were *The Twilight Zone* (1959–1965), *The Outer Limits* (1963–1965), *Voyage to the Bottom of the Sea* (1964–1968), *Lost in Space* (1965–1968), and the original *Star Trek* series (1966–1969), which later inspired spin-off movies and TV series that continue to the present.

TV Becomes International

During the era of the 1960s and 1970s, while the American television industry strove mightily to divert and entertain a vast home audience, the TV medium made huge inroads in foreign lands. Back in the 1940s and 1950s, only a handful of nations outside the United States had attempted to initiate television production and broadcasting. These were all developed countries, mostly in Europe. By 1958 commercial TV existed in twenty-six nations, including Japan, Australia, and a few other non-European countries. But very few TV sets were sold in most of these places before 1960; moreover, far fewer original programs were produced outside America during that period than were made by the big three U.S. networks.

In fact, all of these countries imported at least a few American-made programs during the 1950s. The U.S. networks saw this as a model that might be followed in many other countries that did not yet have television. Clearly the networks could make considerable extra revenue by displaying their shows abroad. To this end, in the 1950s and 1960s NBC helped to fund and set up TV services in West Germany, Sweden, Mexico, Saudi Arabia, Peru, the Philippines, and Kenya. CBS did the same in Greece, India, Liberia, Israel, Argentina, and Venezuela. Likewise, ABC did so in Canada, Guatemala, Colombia, Lebanon, Japan, Australia, and Chile. The American networks provided all of these nations with links to their news departments. They also introduced American programs such as *I Love Lucy, Father Knows Best*, and *Bonanza* to people around the globe. *Bonanza* had become popular in some sixty countries by 1965.

A number of these nations also developed their own local programming, and the experiences of several paralleled those of Britain, the earliest and one of the most successful examples. The British Broadcasting Corporation (BBC) formed in 1922 to manage radio and other emerging electronic communications. It experimented briefly with television in the late 1930s, but World War II halted

TV in the Third World

Television, in the form of one or more broadcasting stations, did not arrive in many third world (poor, nonindustrialized) countries until the 1960s, 1970s, or even later. And even when it did arrive, few people in those nations could afford to buy TV sets. In the late 1950s and early 1960s, for instance, Africa, Asia, and Latin America, with more than seventy countries among them, had less than 3 percent of all the TV sets in the world. In the 1960s and 1970s, several African nations, including Nigeria, Ivory Coast, and Uganda, set up national TV stations. At first these were used mainly to broadcast government propaganda and offered little in the way of entertainment or unbiased news. By 1960 several Middle Eastern countries had TV stations. Among them were Egypt, Lebanon, and Syria. However, most of the imported U.S. programs shown on these stations were censored by the governments, which feared that exposure to Western values would corrupt the people. From the 1960s on, TV audiences in the third world grew by 20 percent a year. Today, about 2.5 to 3 billion people in those countries have access to some kind of television.

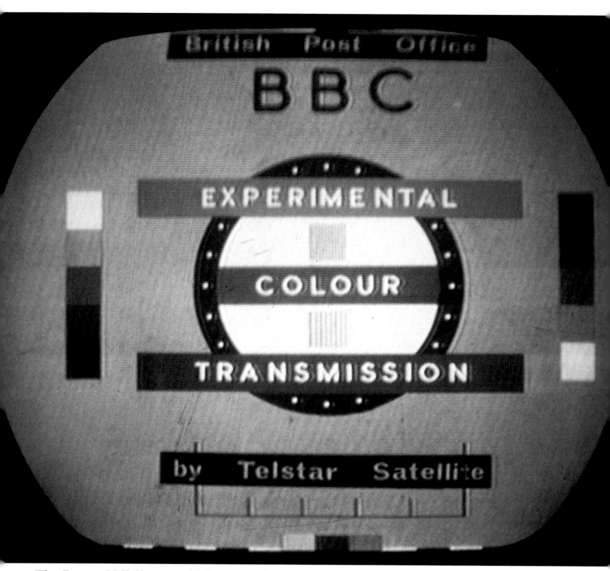

The Benny Hill Show *and* Monty Python's Flying Circus *helped make Britain's BBC one of the most successful international broadcasting companies.*

this activity until 1946. In that year the BBC began regular news broadcasts and aired Britain's first major postwar TV drama, *The Silence of the Sea.*

The audience for these broadcasts was small, however. In 1947 there were only twenty thousand TV sets in Britain, all in London, so most parts of the country saw no television at all. "It was not because people didn't want television," a British observer of that era explained, "but because they could not get it. There were [simply not enough TV sets]. Every dealer had waiting lists and every set that left the manufacturers found its way into a home, but supply fell far short of demand."[39]

The supply of TVs caught up with demand in Britain in the 1950s. But expansion of the country's television industry was slow in that decade, partly because local newspapers and film and theater producers at first saw TV as a competitor and boycotted it. By 1959 the BBC and a second channel, the Independent Television Authority, still provided only sixteen hours of programming per day.

In the 1960s and 1970s, however, television finally came of age in Britain. The number and variety of programs increased. In addition, some British shows of that era, notably *Monty Python's Flying Circus* (1969–1973), went on to gain loyal audiences in the United States and elsewhere. In this way, relentlessly and seemingly inevitably, what had been mainly an American technological and entertainment phenomenon became a global one.

Chapter Four

The Effects of TV on Society

One of the leading historians of television calls it "the most influential social force in American civilization during the second half of the twentieth century."[40] Laurie C. Hillstrom agrees, saying, "Television—and particularly prime-time network series—exerts a tremendous influence on American society." TV affects viewers economically, she points out, influences their perceptions of the world and their political leanings, and helps to shape their daily habits.

TV series encourage people to spend money on toys, clothing, and other products. Television news programs give viewers a close-up look at historic events taking place all over the world. Television coverage of politics influences the type of people who run for office, as well as the ways in which they appeal to voters. Finally, spending time watching television—instead of pursuing other activities like reading, exercising, or talking with other people—affects viewers' personal health and family life.[41]

Everyone agrees that television exerts these and other generalized effects on society. There is less agreement, however, about the degree to which TV influences people's lives. A fair amount of dispute also exists about whether television's effects on society are largely positive or largely negative. Some experts take the middle ground. They argue that TV has both good and bad attributes and that society must do its best to deal with the negative aspects in order to reap the benefits of the positive ones.

Early Predictions About TV and the Family

This difference of opinion has long been particularly marked in regard to televi-

A Painting Acknowledges the Rise of TV

The swift rise of public interest in television and increasing sales of TV sets in the late 1940s were often the subject of other mass media. Particularly noteworthy as a sign of the times was the November 5, 1949, cover of the then–widely popular Saturday Evening Post *magazine. It featured a painting by the famous artist Norman Rockwell, known for his skill in capturing various aspects of American life. The painting, titled* New Television Antenna, *shows an older man watching a younger one attach a TV antenna to the roof of a house. According to a blurb inside the magazine:*

In the Adams street neighborhood of Los Angeles, Norman Rockwell found an ancient house that once upon a time was the newest, snazziest design. That's the way it is in the U.S.A.—today something really new is always being hooked onto what yesterday was the latest thing.

Saturday Evening Post, November 5, 1949, p. 3.

sion's effects on the health, habits, and integrity of the American family. In the early years of mass-marketed commercial TV, many people embraced television and its programming, seeing it as both entertaining and informative. But a few, including some in powerful or influential positions in society, felt that TV viewing was potentially harmful, especially to the fabric of the family and traditional home life. As one early critic put it, "Television began to take over the American living room as a loud-mouthed, sometimes delightful, often shocking, thoroughly unpredictable guest."[42]

Not only was TV brash and invasive, some critics argued, but it also exerted a strong influence on family members' daily habits. It especially affected the rou-tines of children, who were supposedly more susceptible to being manipulated by what they saw on television. One mother warned in 1949, "Television will take over your way of living and change your children's habits."[43] The following year another mother complained, "When the set first came into the house . . . conversation in our home was dead. We ate our suppers in silence, spilling food, gaping in awe. We thought nothing of sitting in the dark for hours at a stretch without exchanging a word."[44] Children would also stop doing their homework and/or become poor students, some critics warned. In 1951 a Catholic archbishop predicted that TV would give children eyestrain, headaches, and "great nervousness and inability to concentrate in

Some early television critics believed that watching television would lead children to neglect their homework and become inattentive in school.

the classroom."[45] In addition, there were fears that children would come to ignore their parents' authority and embrace the values of people they saw on TV.

Children were not the only family members who could potentially be diverted and corrupted by regular TV viewing, early critics cautioned. After seeing partially unclothed female dancers on Jackie Gleason's show and other variety programs, one person suggested, husbands might neglect and cheat on their wives. Likewise, wives might become so addicted to soap op-

eras that they would stop taking care of their families.

In contrast, television broadcasters and TV-set manufacturers believed that television had the potential to bring families together. Members of the new, ideal family they envisioned would spend their leisure hours at home in front of the TV rather than going their separate ways. Supposedly this would foster stronger family relationships.

As the 1950s and 1960s unfolded, neither the gloomy forecasts of the critics nor the rosy ones of TV executives became the norm. Instead, regular television viewing created some new habits and family dynamics that were hard to categorize as either good or bad. Perhaps the biggest change was that both children and adults did come to watch several hours of TV each day; this was time that in the past they would have filled with other pursuits, such as hobbies or outside activities. However, families did not fall apart as a result. People simply adjusted to these changes, thereby creating a somewhat altered state of family normalcy. For instance, most parents made rules about their children's TV viewing, such as ensuring that homework was completed before turning on the set. Similarly, housewives learned to do their chores while taking breaks to catch snippets of their favorite daytime shows. Overall, therefore, as one observer puts it, most Americans "increasingly came to accept TV and to recognize its potentials."[46]

Targeting Family Values and Pocketbooks

The changes wrought by television viewing on family life, whether seen as good, bad, or neutral, occurred in large part because of the rapid growth of suburbia in the years following World War II. Millions of returning soldiers and other young men and women got married and created a demand for affordable single-family homes. Builders responded by creating vast new neighborhoods in the countryside just beyond the limits of the

Religion on Television

One crucial aspect of family life that most early television producers were reluctant to approach was religion. This was mostly out of a fear of offending large groups of viewers. Thus, very few scripted shows depicted outwardly religious or spiritual persons in the first fifty years of American TV. Moreover, those devoutly religious individuals who *were* depicted were either characters in historical or biblical tales or were presented in a very general way, with very little mention of their specific beliefs or rituals. More overt portrayals of religion began in the 1970s with a rash of nonscripted religious programs featuring preachers who used the TV medium as a platform to spread their views. Among many others, these "televangelists," as they came to be called, included Pat Robertson (*The 700 Club*) and Jim and Tammy Faye Bakker (*The PTL Club*). Some of these shows lost viewers when their hosts became involved in financial or sex scandals. Yet several of those who escaped these troubles are still on the air today.

big cities. In their leisure hours, more and more of these suburbanites sought ways to enjoy themselves in the privacy of their homes rather than travel into the cities to seek entertainment. "These couples' desires to invest in a family-focused lifestyle," Edgerton points out, "led them to embrace television entertainment as preferable to traveling downtown to attend movie theaters, as they might have done in previous decades."[47]

To supply this new form of home entertainment, the networks long produced shows that appealed to, and were seen as suitable for viewing by, a general family audience. In the 1950s and well into the 1960s, this approach targeted mostly nuclear, stable, and racially and culturally white families. For the most part, the shows promoted stereotypes, such as all-white neighborhoods, fathers as breadwinners and heads of households, and mothers as housewives and cooks. The characters in these cozy family units interacted "in a warm, loving, comfortable relationship," expert observer Aletha C. Huston writes, "in which there were no major problems, or at least no problems that could not be solved in 30 or 60 minutes. We need only cast our minds back to the Nelsons of *Ozzie and Harriet* or the Andersons of *Father Knows Best* to draw up images of this era."[48]

Such images, however, did not reflect the actual breakdown of families in the nation. Much more diverse, it included divorced couples, single-parent households, families in which the wife or mother worked outside the home, and black, Hispanic, Asian, and other non-white families. Thus, says Huston, "such shows as *Leave It to Beaver* were affirming a view of the family that was not tied to the experiences of most Americans."[49] Beginning in the 1970s, this situation changed. *All in the Family* and other more realistic shows depicted the experiences and problems of a broader range of American families.

In addition to supplying viewers with programming that hopefully would interest but not offend them, the networks and individual TV stations became experts at targeting people's pocketbooks. In order to produce and broadcast their shows, TV producers required the revenue generated by commercials. The idea seemed straightforward enough. A sponsor agreed to back a show and provided ads hawking its product. Viewers saw the ads and went out and bought the product, enriching the sponsor, who used some of the profits to continue backing the show.

This system definitely worked—and continues to work—but one problem often cited by critics is that it does not ensure high-quality programming. A mediocre show sponsored by a popular product might achieve success, for instance, while a higher-quality show is cancelled because too few people buy its sponsor's product. Another drawback frequently cited is that sponsors can, purely for selfish financial reasons, sometimes dictate the sort of programs that get produced. "Most advertisers want to be associated with programs that put people in the mood to spend money and buy their products," Hillstrom writes.

After World War II, a shift to a more family-focused lifestyle led to shows like Leave It to Beaver.

In 1953 the cover of the very first TV Guide *featured Desi Arnaz Jr., the son of TV stars Lucille Ball and Desi Arnaz. Ball appears in the inset photo.*

"For this reason, shows with sad or tragic elements are less likely to appear on TV than those with happy themes."[50]

TV's Wider Impact

Beyond television's effects on family life and habits, the new medium had wide-ranging effects on society as a whole. First, there was a considerable commercial and economic impact, as new, specialized products relating to television were introduced. The "TV dinner" appeared in 1954, for example. This prepackaged meal was designed so that the viewer had only to heat it up for a few minutes before consuming it in front of the TV set. Many TVs were in the living room rather than in the dining room, so "TV trays," small plastic or wooden folding tables, were soon introduced.

Another new and popular product based directly on TV viewing was *TV Guide,* a weekly listing of shows and showtimes, also featuring articles about leading TV personalities. The first issue appeared on April 3, 1953. The cover featured pictures of Lucille Ball, the then-reigning queen of TV sitcoms, and her newborn son, Desi Arnaz Jr. That initial issue sold 1.5 million copies, and by the 1960s *TV Guide* was the most widely circulated magazine in the United States.

In addition to such products, the television industry generated the need for a new, highly specialized professional—the TV repairman. By 1955 there were about one hundred thousand TV repairmen in the country, and the number continued to grow in the years that followed. These technicians found that Americans were so devoted to, and in some cases dependent on, their TVs that most had them fixed within three days of the first sign of malfunction.

Social and economic specialization based on the television medium even extended to house designs. In the 1950s many home builders acknowledged the importance of TV by adding "family rooms" to their blueprints. And many people who had houses custom-built had TVs installed in bedroom or living room walls.

Indeed, for large numbers of Americans, their TV sets became so important as windows into a world of entertainment that other more traditional kinds of entertainment became less popular. By 1951 four times as many people watched television each day as listened to the radio. And moviegoing in America decreased by a whopping 30 percent. Film producers were so worried that they rushed to develop gimmicks designed to lure viewers back into theaters, including the wide-screen process Cinemascope (first unveiled in 1953 with the biblical spectacle *The Robe*).

If TV had the power to alter long-standing moviegoing habits, some argued, it could also potentially affect other sorts of behavior. In particular, a number of prominent individuals and groups worried that watching violent acts on television might make some people more prone to committing such acts. In 1952 Congress held hearings in which several people voiced their concerns about the issue, but no concrete steps were taken to curb TV violence. In 1972 the government released the results of a long-term study that found that "televised violence, indeed, does have an adverse effect on certain members of our society."[51] Children were especially vulnerable to this effect, the study said. But again, no new rules were imposed on the networks. Only after activist groups, such as Action for Children's Television, publicly demanded that something be done did the networks respond. In 1992 they adopted a rating system intended to provide parents with guidance in choosing which programs were suitable for their children to watch. (Among the rating symbols are: TV-Y, meaning a show is suitable for all children; TV-PG, suggesting that parents watch and discuss a show with their children; and TV-MA, indicating a show is for mature adults only.)

The Rise of TV News

The changing habits of some viewers aside, television's greatest single impact on society has arguably been providing average people with information about events in the greater world around them. From the earliest days of regular programming, TV executives recognized a duty to provide the public with daily news shows. At first, these programs were short and fairly unsophisticated. In the 1940s a typical news broadcast lasted only fifteen minutes; a male journalist, who came to be known as the "anchor," sat, facing the camera, and read from a script. NBC's first anchor, radio personality John Cameron Swayze, hit the airwaves in 1948. That same year CBS introduced its first news show with Douglas Edwards as anchor.

These early news shows suffered from a number of disadvantages. One was that the cameras were large and heavy. So it was difficult to transport them to distant locations where news was breaking. Also, these cameras used film, which had to be developed before it could be shown to viewers, further slowing down the news-reporting process.

In spite of these obstacles, the network news departments persevered and made up for their shortcomings by hiring top-notch reporters and commentators. Among them was Edward R. Murrow, who hosted CBS's news commentary show *See It Now* (1951–1955). (NBC had premiered the first news commentary program, *Meet the Press,* in 1947.) Smart, hardworking, bold, and unswervingly fair, Murrow was, in the words of a leading American journalist, "one of those rare legendary figures who was as good as his myth."[52] Murrow believed that TV news should address the country's problems and expose injustice. He most famously put this philosophy into practice in 1954. A powerful Wisconsin senator, Joseph McCarthy, had been holding hearings intended to root out Communists in American society; in several cases he falsely accused people, thereby ruining their careers and lives. On *See It Now,* Murrow courageously exposed McCarthy's bully tactics and abuses of power, and the senator soon lost his support and influence.

Partly because of Murrow and hard-hitting journalists like him, in the 1960s TV news became more professional, comprehensive, and influential. Also, the recently developed medium of videotape was now used instead of film, making news gathering much faster. In addition, communication satellites now made it possible to transmit images of events from around the world almost instantly. Using these new tools, the *CBS Evening News,* with anchor Walter Cronkite, debuted in 1963 and became the gold standard of television news during that era.

Cronkite, whose skills and honesty as a journalist earned him the nickname "the most trusted man in America," was particularly noted for his coverage of several major events of that decade. One was the assassination of President John F. Kennedy in November 1963. A record 90 percent of Americans tuned in to four days of nonstop coverage of the tragedy by Cronkite and other anchors. In this way, "television was at the center of a deeply heartfelt personal experience that most viewers would never forget for the rest of their lives,"[53] Gary R. Edgerton observes.

Does TV News Have Too Much Power?

As the television news departments became increasingly influential during the 1960s and 1970s, some politicians expressed their worries that a few TV executives had gained the power to sway large numbers of citizens and thereby affect the way people voted in elections. Among these critics was Vice President Spiro Agnew, who stated in November 1969:

At least 40 million Americans every night, it's estimated, watch the network news. . . . According to Harris polls and other studies, for millions of Americans the networks are the sole source of national and world news. In [famous humorist] Will Roger's observation, what you knew was what you read in the newspaper. Today for growing millions of Americans, it's what they see and hear on their television sets. Now how is this network news determined? A small group of men, numbering perhaps no more than a dozen anchormen, commentators, and executive producers, settle upon the 20 minutes or so of film and commentary that's to reach the public. . . . Their powers of choice are broad. They decide what 40 to 50 million Americans will learn of the day's events in the nation and in the world. We cannot measure this power and influence by the traditional democratic standards, for these men can create national issues overnight.

Quoted in American Rhetoric, "Spiro Theodore Agnew: Television News Coverage." www.american rhetoric.com/speeches/spiroagnewtvnewscoverage.htm.

TV news in the 1960s became increasingly influential, and news anchor Walter Cronkite was called "the most trusted man in America."

Other important news stories that TV news organizations thoroughly covered in the years that followed included highlights of the civil rights movement, including the murder of Martin Luther King Jr.; the Vietnam War, which came to be called the first "TV war"; and the successful landing of American astronauts on the moon in 1969.

Television and Politics

Another way that TV news has strongly affected American society (as well as British and other foreign societies) is by televising political events; these include campaigns and elections as well as the life and work of politicians. The Democratic and Republican parties began airing their national conventions on TV in 1948, giving large numbers of Americans the feeling of "being there." But the real power of television to sway public political opinion first became clear in the 1952 election. Republican candidate Dwight D. Eisenhower aired several thirty-second campaign ads that experts called critical to his subsequent victory.

Television affected politics in a different way that same year. Eisenhower's running mate, Richard M. Nixon, was accused of accepting illegal gifts from donors. Nixon shrewdly gave a speech on TV denying any improper actions, a broadcast watched by some 60 million Americans. The speech saved his candidacy. However, the power of TV had the opposite effect on Nixon when he ran for president eight years later. In widely televised debates with Democratic candidate John F. Kennedy, the camera captured Nixon's stiffness and nervousness, contributing to Kennedy's ultimate win.

In the 1960s and 1970s, some politicians and other powerful individuals complained that television broadcasters and commentators had come to exert too much influence on the public. One of the better-known attacks on that influence was by Vice President Spiro Agnew (served 1969 to 1973). He called network executives and news managers "a small, unelected elite," who could "reward some politicians with national exposure and ignore others."[54] Some saw Agnew's tirade as nothing more than a bitter partisan attack. Yet others pointed out a grain of truth in the speech, namely that television had come to exert an enormous influence not only over American politics but also over nearly every other aspect of society.

Chapter Five

The Dawn of the Cable Era

The period beginning in the late 1970s and ending in the early 1990s witnessed a revolution in the television industry almost as big as the social revolution created by TV itself in the 1940s and 1950s. Before the 1970s, the "big three" American networks—NBC, CBS, and ABC—had enjoyed a near monopoly on television programming and broadcasting. They had made TV a huge business tightly controlled by themselves. Few in the industry expected them to face any serious challenges from would-be competitors in the foreseeable future.

In the 1970s, however, the first of these competitors—consisting of several TV cable companies—boldly made their bid for part of the lucrative TV distribution market. Cable systems had been around since the 1940s, but they had long been small and had merely carried the networks' programs to rural areas with poor reception of airborne television signals.

As long as the cable companies produced no original programming of their own, they posed no threat to the big networks. Eventually, though, cable reached so many homes that a few enterprising individuals saw the potential to create their own programs and try to grab a slice of the big networks' pie.

The so-called cable TV era that resulted would be more accurately termed the *cable and satellite TV era*. This is because satellites capable of receiving and transmitting television signals appeared in the 1960s. Such satellites made the wide distribution of cable signals possible. Before feeding signals via wires to customers spaced over large distances, a cable company had to have a link to a central signal carrying its programs. One or more satellites provided that link. A cable channel broadcast its signal to a satellite, which then transmitted it to cable substations across the country. Thus, as University of Wisconsin scholar

Michele Hilmes puts it, "satellite transmission turned cable from a local to a national, even global, medium."[55]

This powerful technological alliance of cable and satellites profoundly changed the face of TV. No longer did viewers have only three or four basic packages of programming from which to choose. Now people with enough money, ambition, and innovative ideas could start their own cable channel or network and produce their own shows. Moreover, they could afford to target more specific groups of viewers with more specific tastes and wants. A cable provider could create its own TV niche, for instance, by airing only cooking shows, horse-racing events, or educational shows. This not only gave viewers many more programming choices, but it also launched what some have called niche TV or genre TV, characterized by specialized programming.

The Growth of Cable TV

The first cable TV systems in the United States were installed in 1948 and 1949 in two widely separated rural towns—Lansford, Pennsylvania, and Astoria, Oregon. In the case of Lansford, few of its residents had purchased TVs, mainly because their reception was poor. The nearest television broadcasting station was in Philadelphia, 65 miles (105km) away, and a mountain near Lansford blocked the already weak signal. To get around these obstacles, some local investors pooled

Movies on Television

The big three TV networks, NBC, CBS, and ABC, have always shown full-length movies, not only in prime time but also during the daytime and on what used to be called the late, late show, from 11:30 P.M. to 3:00 A.M. As time went on, it was not only theatrical films that made it onto TV. In the 1960s and 1970s the networks began making movies of their own, which came to called made-for-TV movies. The peak of network movie presentations, including both theatrical and made-for-TV movies, occurred in 1973. During that year the three major networks aired about 19.5 hours of movies per week in prime time alone. Among the leading shows in this genre were *The ABC Sunday Night Movie*, *The NBC Mystery Movie*, and *The Tuesday Night CBS Movie*. In the 1980s, however, viewers' tastes for TV movies rapidly began to change. First, HBO and other cable networks began showing many movies uncut and uncensored, drawing some viewers away from the big networks. Also, the advent of affordable VCRs allowed viewers to rent whichever movies they wanted, including some that were too "racy" to be shown on network TV.

their resources and erected a TV tower atop the mountain. The tower picked up the signal from Philadelphia, diverted it into an amplifier (to strengthen it), and then fed it into coaxial cables, which carried it to local homes. A coaxial cable is a copper wire coated with insulation and aluminum sheathing on the outside. Such cables had already been used to carry telephone signals.

Once the new cable system went into operation, Lansford's TV viewers received the same programs, with the same visual and audio quality, as Philadelphia viewers did. The main difference was that people in the big city received the signals for free, whereas Lansford's residents had to pay three dollars per month. For this reason, cable TV systems were often referred to in those days as pay TV.

For several years afterward, cable systems remained few in number and primarily served the needs of rural communities that got substandard reception from urban TV stations. In 1950 the country had a mere 70 such systems, with 14,000 subscribers. And there were just 650 cable systems with 650,000 subscribers in 1960. At that time, with more than 45 million TV owners in existence in the United States, those receiving cable programming made up only one-seventieth of the total. However, over the next two decades the number of cable systems and subscribers grew substantially. In 1970 there

The technological partnership between cable and satellites created the cable industry and forever changed television.

were 2,500 cable systems serving 4.5 million viewers; by 1985 these numbers had increased to 6,600 systems and 40 million viewers.

As the cable TV industry grew, some local cable organizations began to show more than the standard network shows. At first, some cable systems expanded their programming by carrying locally produced shows from distant cities. Later, the largest cable companies began producing their own shows. Not surprisingly, the big three networks were alarmed, fearing that competition from cable TV would hurt their bottom line. They appealed to the Federal Communications Commission (FCC), which at first supported them by tightly regulating what local cable companies could show. But over time the cable industry fought back. It appealed not only to the FCC but also to Congress, demanding that it be allowed to compete fairly with the traditional broadcast networks. Responding to this pressure, in 1984 Congress passed the Cable Communications Policy Act (sponsored by Arizona senator Barry Goldwater). This legislation removed almost all regulations on cable TV, making it, legally speaking, the equal of the big three networks.

The 1980s therefore witnessed the emergence of what were in effect many new television networks, all of which provided their programs through the cable medium. The number of cable networks grew from twenty-eight in 1980 to an impressive seventy-nine in 1990. Among the more successful at first were HBO (Home Box Office), which initially showed only theatrical movies; and Ted Turner's TBS (Turner Broadcasting System), which came to provide a mix of movies, sports, and news. ESPN (specializing in sports) and MTV (creating a niche for popular music) were also successful.

The Impact of Cable News

Also in the 1980s, Ted Turner launched the Cable News Network (CNN), designed to carry news programs twenty-four hours a day. This was an unusual and controversial concept at the time. Some critics questioned whether there was enough news to fill all those hours. They charged that CNN spent too much time covering "fluff" such as the legal troubles and trials of celebrities. Others criticized CNN's initial low budget, which resulted in a simplistic, spare look, especially when compared to the big three networks' elaborate sets and slick operations.

Despite these criticisms, CNN slowly but steadily attracted more viewers and started making a profit. A large boost came when the U.S. space shuttle *Challenger* exploded shortly after takeoff in 1986. At the time CNN was the only major news organization covering the launch, so it scored an enormous news scoop. An even bigger ratings bonanza occurred in 1991 at the start of the Persian Gulf War. (The United States sent troops to Iraq to force its dictator, Saddam Hussein, to remove his forces from neighboring Kuwait, which he had recently invaded.) On the night in which U.S planes began bombing Iraq's capital, Baghdad, three CNN reporters, Peter Arnett, Bernard Shaw, and John Holliman, broadcast the spectacle live from the balcony of their Baghdad hotel room. Millions of viewers tuned in. Thereafter, CNN had a reputation for transmitting major breaking stories as they unfolded. Still another exclusive for CNN developed when Hussein ordered all foreign journalists to leave Iraq; the only exception was Peter Arnett. He continued to cover the war from the inside. Thanks to these and other efforts, by 1996 CNN was making more money than the news divisions of NBC, CBS, and ABC combined.

CNN also began broadcasting via satellite from and to major cities around the world. This made it the first truly international TV network. To emphasize the concept that events and news in one part of the globe often affect the other parts, Turner was careful not to make his company look like an American operation attempting to dominate the world news market. Rather, CNN portrayed itself as a sort of news outlet for a global community. "Even today," Gary R. Edgerton points out,

CNN, the Cable News Network, carries news programming twenty-four hours a day.

CNN employees are not permitted to use the word "foreign" to describe international viewers, guests, or issues. Ted Turner learned early what cable content providers take for granted today—good content will attract viewers regardless of territorial boundaries or nationality.[56]

Turner was not the only successful provider of cable news. Others followed his lead, including one of the traditional networks, NBC, which created a separate cable news division—MSNBC. The Fox cable network, owned by controversial Australian mogul Rupert Murdock, spun off the twenty-four-hour Fox News Channel. As a result, cable news became the news venue that most Americans relied on for information. By 2001 polls showed that about 45 percent of TV viewers got their news from cable, compared with just 22 percent who got it from the big three networks' nightly news programs. (The rest relied on either local TV news programs or newspapers.)

Other New Technologies

Along with the coaxial cable and the cable TV systems that utilized it, a number of other new technologies and devices enhanced the TV-viewing experience between the 1970s and 1990s. One was satellite TV. Bell Laboratories, AT&T, and NASA had joined forces to launch the first communications satellite, TELSTAR, in 1962. That same year it broadcast a live TV show across the Atlantic Ocean (from Maryland to France) for the first time. Such satellites

made it possible to relay images across the globe almost instantly, and this is how hundreds of millions of people worldwide watched U.S. astronauts land on the Moon, in real time, in 1969.

However, for a long time satellites relayed only the signals created by the big three networks and later by various cable TV companies. Satellites did not normally transmit directly to people's homes. Eventually, however, some innovative and ambitious individuals saw the potential for doing just that, thereby eliminating the so-called middleman of cable. In 1990 Primestar became the first company to provide satellite TV service directly to viewers' homes. Each home was required to lease a 3-foot-wide (1m) "dish" antenna to receive the signals.

This new technology presented stiff competition for the cable TV companies. In response, in 1994 they persuaded Congress to pass the Satellite Home Viewer Act, which limited the ability of satellite systems to broadcast certain cable and network shows. However, thanks to pressure from citizen groups, Congress reversed itself in 1999. Now having the right to compete directly with cable, satellite TV systems rapidly expanded, reaching 17.4 million subscribers by 2001 (compared with 8.2 million in 1998).

Another technological breakthrough that enhanced TV broadcasting and viewing was the fiber-optic cable. First developed by the Corning chemical company in 1970, it consists of clear glass or plastic rods that transmit information on rapid pulses of light. A fiber-optic cable can carry an astounding

The Impact of Shooting on Tape

Most of the early television shows of the late 1940s and early 1950s were either shot on film or presented live in a studio. Milton Berle's variety show and other programs like it were live shows, for instance. Most of these live shows were produced by individuals directly hired and overseen by the shows' sponsors. This gave the sponsors a great deal of control over content, including the subjects of the shows, the dialogue, the casting, and so forth. When videotape became available in the mid-1950s, however, the situation swiftly changed. With the ability to shoot on tape, anyone could produce a TV show and could do so almost anywhere. As a result, most television production companies moved to the Los Angeles area to take advantage of the talent available in the Hollywood community. In addition, the networks took almost complete charge of their own shows, leaving the sponsors with the simpler role of either agreeing or disagreeing to back a particular show.

sixty-five thousand times more information than a copper wire. By the 1980s and 1990s, fiber optics allowed TV providers to transmit large numbers of channels in a single cable.

No less significant was the advent of the videocassette recorder (VCR). Videotape had been around since the 1950s, when it allowed television producers to record their programs faster and cheaper than they could with film. But for a long time the public had no access to this technology; this was largely because the original equipment was large, bulky, and very expensive. The situation began to change when the Phillips Corporation introduced the first home VCR in 1972. Sony, RCA, and other companies released their own versions in the years that followed. In turn, the price of these

devices steadily came down, inducing tens of millions of viewers to buy them. As a result, Barbara Moore writes,

in a relatively short period of time, VCRs changed the way people watch television. Programs could be time-shifted (recorded for later viewing at a more convenient time) and commercials zipped (sped through) or zapped (not recorded), a major change in which it is the viewers who determine what and when to watch, not the television networks or their local affiliates.[57]

More Choices for Viewers

One of the more important aspects of the spread of new broadcast and recording

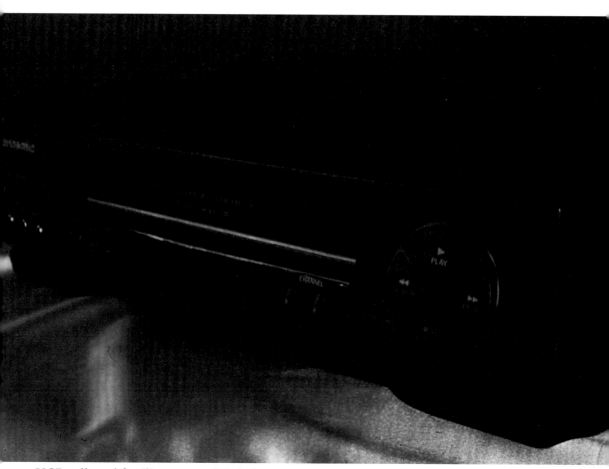

VCRs allowed families to record their favorite TV shows for later viewing.

technologies such as cable, satellite, and VCRs was providing television viewers with far more choices than ever before. In the 1980s and 1990s, Laurie C. Hillstrom points out,

> instead of the four or five broadcast channel options that were previously available, American viewers suddenly had up to fifty cable [and satellite] channels from which to choose. . . . This change in focus led to more experimentation [in TV production] and greater diversity of programs.[58]

Not all of the shows produced during this burst of diversity were high quality or popular, but more than a few were. Still competitive, the traditional big three networks continued to turn out a number of high-budget shows that attracted large home audiences. One of the more successful of these programs was CBS's *Dallas* (1978–1991). The ongoing dramatic saga of a wealthy Texas oil family,

The TV series Dallas *brought the soap opera format to prime time.*

it starred Larry Hagman (formerly of *I Dream of Jeannie*) as the ruthless tycoon J.R. Ewing, who both the other characters and viewers loved to hate.

The show was notable partly because it effectively brought the daytime soap opera format and style to prime time. Like the daytime version, it had many interacting characters in a continuing story line, complete with cliff-hangers at the end of each episode. Other networks were quick to copy this winning formula. Successful prime-time soaps of the era included *Knots Landing* (1979–1993), *Dynasty* (1981–1989), and *Falcon Crest* (1981–1990). These shows about the inner workings of rich families were also noteworthy because they reflected the popular big-business mentality of American culture in the 1980s. In addition, they attracted large audiences because they explored the same personal family problems that many Americans dealt with but were sometimes reluctant to talk about. Thus, as Moore puts it, "Marriages, affairs, pregnancies, divorces, and remarriages took place; identities were mistaken . . . business empires were built and collapsed . . . scandals tore families asunder; and [there were also] murders, rapes, and kidnappings."[59]

Dallas and most other big three network shows aimed to draw the biggest cross-sections of the American public as possible. In contrast, meanwhile, the newer cable networks targeted smaller but very loyal and reliable audiences with niche-oriented programming. Fox scored a sizable hit with *The X-Files* (1993–2002), for instance. It was an offbeat genre piece about two FBI agents who regularly encounter strange, paranormal, and at times terrifying phenomena. Fox producers and executives were well aware that the show would not appeal to a wide audience. But, as Moore explains, it "had a dark look, scary special effects, and a pervasive atmosphere of paranoia that created a loyal group of fans."[60] Those same fans later ensured the success of two spin-off theatrical movies based on the series.

Another example of niche programming that tapped into a small but loyal audience was (and remains) the incredible success of the *Star Trek* franchise. When the original series (with William Shatner as Captain Kirk) appeared in the 1960s, it was cancelled after only seventy-nine episodes. This was mainly because in those days genre shows, including science fiction ones like *Star Trek*, were usually unable to gain a large enough share of America's viewing audience to satisfy their corporate sponsors. In the 1980s and 1990s, however, with genre shows multiplying and thriving, several new *Star Trek* series appeared; these included *Star Trek: The Next Generation* (1987–1994), *Star Trek: Deep Space Nine* (1993–1999), and *Star Trek: Voyager* (1995–2001). (In addition, numerous successful *Star Trek* motion pictures were released in the 1980s and 1990s.) Other niche programs that effectively targeted specific sectors of the viewing audience in that era included *Thirtysomething* (1987–1991), which appealed to young, upwardly mobile adults; *Lois and Clark: The New Adventures of Superman* (1993–1997), which attracted adventure and comic-book fans; and *Beverly*

Roddenberry's "Wagon Train to the Stars"

Jack Kelly of American Heritage *magazine tells how the original* Star Trek *show got started in the 1960s:*

E arly television had seen a few science fiction series . . . but the genre didn't seem well suited to the small screen. Production costs were high, and the stories were often weird. Studios liked simple, inexpensive sets; viewers liked familiarity. Gene Roddenberry, a journeyman television writer who had worked on Westerns like *Have Gun, Will Travel*, conceived *Star Trek* as a way to overcome these limits. It would be *"Wagon Train* to the stars," he declared. Weekly plots drawn from all over the galaxy would play out mainly within the confines of the *Enterprise*, so the sets could be used over and over. . . . Still, the show would be expensive, and Roddenberry was lucky to sell the concept to Lucille Ball's Desilu studio, which induced NBC to broadcast it. Many fans . . . responded to the overt tolerance that reigned aboard the *Enterprise*. . . . "Leave any bigotry in your quarters, mister," Captain Kirk tells a crew member. "There's no room for it on the bridge." Roddenberry fought with censors to include the first interracial kiss ever shown on television, between Kirk [the ship's captain] and Uhura [the communications officer].

Jack Kelly, "*Star Trek*'s Slow Start,"AmericanHeritage.com, September 7, 2006. www.americanheritage .com/entertainment/articles/web/20060907-star-trek-william-shatner-television-sci-fi.shtml.

Hills 90210 (1990–2000), which gained a loyal audience of teenagers.

New, Innovative Sitcoms

The one programming genre that retained wide popularity across the board, from the big three networks to the cable networks, was the ever-durable sitcom. With the huge success of dramatic shows like *Dallas* in the early 1980s, for a while it appeared that sitcoms were on the wane. However, situation comedies enjoyed a new lease on life thanks in large part to the major success of Bill Cosby's *The Cosby Show* (1984–1992). Long a popular comedian, Cosby had scored an early success in television with his espionage-themed show *I Spy*, which ran from 1965 to 1968 and earned him three Emmy awards. His new 1980s sitcom, which portrayed the exploits of an upper-middle-class African American family, was even more popular. It soared to the top of the TV ratings for four years in a row and won several Emmys.

Some critics faulted the show for supposedly presenting an atypical picture of black life in America. Most blacks were

The Cosby Show *paved the way for other smartly written sitcoms that portrayed family life somewhat more realistically.*

not financially successful like the Huxtables on *The Cosby Show*, the critics charged. Likewise, the show rarely addressed the experiences and problems of lower-class blacks. However, the show's enormous popularity in other countries revealed how shortsighted these attacks were and how truly innovative and progressive the show really was. "Throughout the 1980s," Edgerton explains,

> *The Cosby Show* consistently topped the ratings in Canada, Australia, New Zealand [and across Europe]. The series made accessible to viewers an African American upper-class lifestyle that had been around for centuries but rarely got noticed by popular culture. In fact, the main political work of the show was this effort to uncouple portrayals of African Americans from their prior connections with poverty and popular youth culture. In this way, the series [achieved] a comparatively dignified depiction of African Americans shorn of conventional reliance on black stereotypes.[61]

Another notable achievement of *The Cosby Show* was to revive interest among both viewers and producers in smartly written sitcoms that realistically yet humorously depicted the dynamics of diverse kinds of American families. *Roseanne* (1988–1997), starring saucy female comic Roseanne Barr, was one of the more successful. Other popular entries in the genre included *The Wonder Years* (1988–1993), *The Fresh Prince of Bel-Air* (1990–1996), *Home Improvement* (1991–1999), and *Frasier* (1994–2004, a spin-off of another popular comedy, *Cheers*, which ran from 1983 to 1993). These shows added to the wide range of TV offerings that existed by the early 1990s. But though American television viewers now had access to more numerous and diverse choices than ever before, they would find these a mere foretaste of even more astonishing variety to come.

Chapter Six

A Channel for Everyone

By the early 1990s a new television landscape had emerged in the United States (and in Britain, Japan, and other nations whose TV industries followed similar trends). Familiar to today's viewers because it is still in place, that landscape has been characterized in part by a major decline in the power of the big three networks. As late as the 1978–1979 TV season, NBC, CBS, and ABC provided a total of 91 percent of television's prime-time shows. By 1986–1987, however, that number had decreased to 75 percent. And by 1993–1994 it was down to 61 percent.

Several factors contributed to this decline in the market share and influence of the big networks. One factor has been the continued spread of VCR players and the wide proliferation of rental stores (such as Blockbuster Video) carrying videotapes of movies and TV shows. Some 72 percent of U.S. homes had VCRs by 1991 (compared with only 4 percent in 1982).

By 2000 85 percent of homes had them. Some people simply reduced their network TV viewing in favor of watching movies and other videos on their VCRs.

A much bigger factor in the decline of the traditional networks has been the continued success of cable and satellite TV systems. In recent years, these technologies have expanded niche programming into an almost bewildering array of hundreds of new networks (often referred to as channels). As in the case of earlier genre shows, each appeals to a limited but enthusiastic and loyal audience. The History Channel, the Discovery Channel, Animal Planet, the National Geographic Channel, Lifetime, Nickelodeon, C-Span, the Weather Channel, the Food Network, the Science Fiction Channel, the Cartoon Network, the Warner Brothers (WB) Network, and the United Paramount Network (UPN) have been only a few of the more prominent examples. (In 2006 the WB and UPN merged to form the CW Network.) Of these and the many other cable and satellite channels available, the Discovery Channel was the highest rated in 2008, with about 98 million regular viewers.

Partly because of the tremendous variety of channels available, the remote-control keypad also came to play a significant role in both TV watching and the decline of the big network's share of viewers. The remote control was invented in the 1950s, but it did not become commonplace in homes until the 1980s and 1990s. By 1991, a survey found that 37 percent of viewers regularly "channel surfed" rather than watching a single program from start to finish. Thus, if someone was bored with an ABC or CBS show, he or she might instantly switch to one or more cable or satellite programs. "Consumers at home were slowly becoming more proactive [hands-on] in their TV viewing behavior," Edgerton notes. Meanwhile, "their adoption of these new television-related accessories aided in the industry's wholesale transition from broadcasting to narrowcasting."[62]

Digital and Other New Technologies

The remote control is only one of many such TV-related accessories and devices in what some have come to call the digital age of television (and other electronic media). The word *digital* refers to the manner in which images and sounds are recorded and then shown on a TV (or a computer or other electronic device). Before the 1990s, nearly all television signals were broadcast in a system known as analog. In simple terms, an analog signal is one in which the images and sounds correspond to slight variations in radio waves traveling through the air or a cable. Analog signals can carry a certain set amount of tiny bits of information; therefore, they produce a set amount of resolution, or detail and sharpness, on a TV screen. That amount of resolution was acceptable in prior decades, when technology was less advanced. However, as one expert observer notes,

> The worst computer monitors you can buy [today] have more resolution than the best analog TV set; and the best computer monitors are able to display up to 10 times more [detail] than that TV set. There is simply no comparison between a computer monitor and an analog TV in terms of detail, crispness, image stability and color.

The images on a computer monitor possess more detail and are crisper looking and more stable because they are digital rather than analog. Digital images are made up of thousands of color dots, known as pixels. Within these pixels are long strands of digital information (represented as 1s and 0s) that allow for greater resolution. Thus, the same observer notes, "the drive toward digital TV is fueled by the desire to give TV the same crispness and detail as a computer screen."[63]

Beginning in the 1990s, many television providers began delivering their signals in digital. However, they still delivered them in analog as well because most people's TV sets could only display analog. (Newer sets were equipped with digital capacity.) The FCC eventually set a transition date for early 2009; thereafter all television providers would be required to broadcast in digital only. This decision was based partly on the fact that analog signals take up four times as much space in the airwaves as more compact digital signals do. (In other words, a station can broadcast four digital TV shows in the same amount of airspace as one analog show.)

In the meantime, the digital revolution was generating other devices that many TV viewers readily bought. In 2000 digital video discs (DVDs), which record images and sounds on compact discs rather than on tape, hit the market in a big way. The following year most movie studios began releasing their films on DVD as well as on videotape. By 2004 DVDs of both movies and popular TV shows began outselling the videotape versions. Also, more and more television networks started showing digital versions of their shows online (after they had already been aired on TV) for the benefit of those viewers who had missed an episode of a favorite program.

In this same period, stores began carrying new kinds of TV sets that do not employ the traditional cathode-ray tube. Among the more popular of these types are liquid crystal display (LCD) TVs and plasma TVs. In an LCD TV, light passes through a panel containing many tiny liquid crystals; a light source behind the panel illuminates the crystals. By contrast, images on a plasma TV are produced by hundreds of tiny cells containing xenon and neon gas. An electrical current causes the gases to emit light. Both LCD and plasma technology allow for thin, relatively lightweight screens with bright, crisp images. The technology also allows

Digital televisions bring a crisper, more detailed picture to viewers.

Family Sitcoms Are Still Popular

Although many of the sitcoms of the 1990s were aimed at single people, a few stayed with the tried-and-true family comedy format that had long been successful. One of the more successful of these efforts was *Everybody Loves Raymond*, which debuted in 1996. It was based loosely on the family experiences of its star and namesake, popular comedian Ray Romano. Most of the show's humorous situations revolved around Ray's parents, who frequently interfered with his home life. Another widely popular family sitcom of that decade featured cartoon rather than real-life actors. *The Simpsons*, which premiered in 1990, chronicles the exploits of a dysfunctional urban family headed by the clumsy, inept Homer Simpson. Large numbers of viewers loved the show, perhaps because beneath the surface it advocated family togetherness. As one observer puts it, "Despite criticisms of the program as flouting traditional family values, many episodes underscore their strength as an intact family. Through all of their surrealistic adventures, they remain together."

Barbara Moore et al., *Prime-Time Television: A Concise History.* London: Praeger, 2006, pp. 245–46.

for larger screens than in the past, and big-screen TVs have become increasingly popular. These TVs were relatively expensive at first, but their prices came down steadily as demand grew. By 2005 a 42-inch (107-cm) plasma set retailed for about fourteen hundred dollars. In the years that followed, prices dropped further.

Targeting the Youth Market

As the digital revolution gained steam, competition among the numerous TV networks became stiffer than ever. Virtually all, including the traditional big three, now attempted to target various viewer niches, some fairly modest in scope, others more ambitious. One of the largest and most lucrative groups of viewers (from the standpoint of their potential to buy the sponsors' products) was the so-called youth market. Some experts break it down into two subgroups or demographics (specific portions of the population). One subgroup, "teens," includes people ranging in age from about twelve to twenty. When *Beverly Hills 90210* became a big hit on Fox in the 1990s, other networks tried to compete by creating their own shows featuring teenagers. Fox also successfully targeted the other youth subgroup, "young adults" (aged eighteen to thirty-four). Its prime-time young adult soaps *Melrose Place* (1992–1999) and *Party of Five* (1994–2000) were both highly successful.

A Launching Pad for Comedy Stars

One of the most innovative and popular series in TV history—*Saturday Night Live*, often called more simply *SNL*—has also been a launching pad and proving ground for numerous comedians and actors who later became big TV or motion-picture stars. A partial list of the *SNL* cast members who went on to stardom includes Chevy Chase, Billy Crystal, Bill Murray, Martin Short, Dana Carvey, Mike Myers, Will Ferrell, and Tina Fey. Each week, beginning with the show's premiere in 1975, one or more of these stars, along with others in a regular cast of players, have appeared in a series of comedy sketches. These skits have often pushed the boundaries of television by presenting controversial topics and at times racy language. (Mostly the show has escaped censorship because it is broadcast at 11:30 P.M., when children are supposed to be asleep.)

Various networks also produced new, innovative sitcoms designed to tap into the youth market. For the most part, these were aimed at young single people, a significant departure from the recent rash of family-oriented sitcoms. The leading entry in this genre, in artistic quality as well as popularity, was *Seinfeld* (1990–1998). Starring popular stand-up comic Jerry Seinfeld, it featured one of the most original, and in some ways daring, formats in television comedy history. Seinfeld and his three closest friends "lived in New York City and were basically selfish people," as one TV historian summarizes it.

Unlike many of us, though, they felt no guilt at being self-centered and were only mildly embarrassed when their shallowness was exposed. Most of the show's topics dealt with small questions about the manners and mores of the time, which led to its description as "the show about nothing." After a slow start, the show reached cult status. The audience seemed to identify with characters who weren't villains, but could be considered antiheroes on a petty scale.[64]

Another youth-oriented show that drew a large audience at the dawn of the digital age was NBC's *Friends* (1994–2004). It was built around six close friends in their twenties who frequent a coffee house in New York City. Perhaps hoping to appeal to both teens and young adults, the show's writers often placed the friends in juvenile situations and peppered the dialogue with current pop-culture references.

The 2000s and Reality TV

NBC was happy to have a hit show like *Friends,* of course. But for each such hit that a large network scored, it aired many shows that attracted few viewers and lasted only one season or even less. Moreover, most of these scripted shows with recognizable actors were very expensive to produce. By 2003, for instance, each episode of *Friends* cost about $10 million.

With so many networks competing for the attention of a more or less fixed number of viewers, the bigger networks avidly searched for ways to cut costs.

One solution to this dilemma turned out to be the so-called reality show, so named because it features "real" people rather than trained actors; also, these people are placed in supposedly real situations instead of scripted or fictional ones.

In a departure from family-oriented shows, Seinfeld, *shown here, and* Friends *were aimed at young singles.*

Fox's American Idol *is one of the most successful reality shows on television.*

One benefit for the networks is that the participants do not have to be paid high salaries, as named actors do. Also, there are no expensive sets or special effects in reality shows. Thus, a typical reality show can be produced for a fraction of the cost of the least expensive scripted show.

Reality shows were not new to the 2000s. They had existed for decades in one form or another, one being the game show, which features average people competing for prizes. *Candid Camera* (1948–1967), in which real people were placed in odd situations and secretly filmed, was perhaps the most famous example from times past. Two very popular reality shows of the 1990s—*The Real World* and *America's Funniest Home Videos*—became the inspiration for the veritable explosion of reality shows to come.

The show that launched that new wave of reality TV in 2000 was CBS's *Survivor*. Sixteen strangers were taken to a remote island in the South China Sea, where they had to find food, build shelters, and survive for several weeks without the benefit of modern conveniences. They also met periodically to vote one of their members off the island; the last person left on the island received a $1 million prize. *Survivor* struck a nerve with the public and was so popular that its season finale was second only to football's Super Bowl in the TV ratings.

Not surprisingly, there followed an onrush of reality shows on a wide variety of networks. By 2002, five of the ten most popular shows on the air were reality shows. By 2004, almost 40 percent of all shows on American television were in the reality category. Among the more successful were Fox's *American Idol,* consisting of a series of auditions for young singers hoping to garner a recording contract; *The Apprentice,* in which multimillionaire Donald Trump auditions potential business assistants (and each week tells one of them "You're fired!"); and ABC's *Extreme Makeover: Home Edition,* in which volunteers build new homes for needy families. The latter was one of the few reality shows

that critics praised rather than panned as lowbrow or fluff. In 2004 the Parents Television Council called *Extreme Makeover* "an excellent example of a constructive and uplifting reality show. Unlike other reality series that emphasize and exploit contestants' worst qualities (greed, dishonesty, vanity, etc.), this inspiring program showcases charity and selflessness."[65]

The Networks Go After Adults

Another aspect of the sometimes cutthroat competition among the TV networks involved so-called adult content. This included not only mature or controversial themes but also the use of nudity, crude language, and/or extreme violence on the air. People pay for cable and therefore elect to receive the shows they want; so it has long been assumed in the industry that they do not mind seeing, and in fact often desire to see, such adult content. As a result, it became customary for cable networks like HBO to include more violence and nudity and in general more adult themes in their programs.

As the digital age was beginning, the noncable networks realized that they were losing many adult viewers to cable and had to try to recapture them. This was a major motivation behind ABC's police drama *NYPD Blue* (1993–2004). Because of its brief nude scenes (mostly showing characters' rear ends) and explicit language, 25 percent of ABC's local stations at first refused to air the show. But it became a big hit with viewers. This was partly because they liked the complex characters and gritty realism of the

Is Watching Disasters on Television Stressful?

Although no definitive answer exists for the question above, the journal Psychological Science *researched this topic for its April 2007 issue. The journal reported on a study of how TV viewing of the 9/11 disaster in 2001 affected the mental health of college-age individuals. Those who conducted the study looked at the "dream journals" kept by several students in a college psychology class.*

According to the online health directory PsychCentral:

The study data finds that for every hour of television viewed on Sept. 11, with some students reporting in excess of 13 hours watched, levels of stress, as indicated by dream content, increased significantly. In addition, the study found that time spent talking with family and friends helped individuals to better process the day's horrific events. The questionnaire responses showed that throughout the day of Sept. 11, students spent between . . . 1.5 and 13 hours watching television news coverage of the attacks, an average of 6.5 hours. . . . The authors found that the greater the amount of time students spent talking about the 9/11 events with family and friends, the greater the likelihood their dreams contained "thematic" images, rather than specific images.

Rick Nauert, "TV Coverage of Disaster Can Increase Stress," PsychCentral. http://psychcentral.com/news/2007/04/17/tv-coverage-of-disaster-can-increase-stress.

urban New York settings. "After the shock [of the nude scenes] wore off," Barbara Moore remarks,

viewers became interested in characters like Andy Sipowicz (Dennis Franz), an officer with a tough beat and a tougher attitude and a personal life that seemed more appropriate for a soap opera. He went through a number of partners, both professional and romantic, and the audience stayed fascinated with the series.[66]

Another big network offering that went after adult viewers was *Law and Order* (1990–), currently the longest-running prime-time drama still producing new episodes. The show deals with mature adult themes and features a fair amount of violence; but its trademark is the way it traces a legal case from the crime to the arrest of the perpetrator to his or her court trial. Also, many of the show's stories have been inspired by real cases. The wide popularity of the show led to some equally popular spin-offs, including *Law and Order: Criminal Intent* and *Law and Order: Special Victim's Unit*, both still on the air in 2009. Other successful adult-oriented network shows have been CBS's *CSI: Crime Scene Investigation* (2000–) and ABC's *Lost* (2004–) and *Desperate Housewives* (2004–).

Cable Scores Some Big Hits

Rather than being outdone by the big networks' adult-oriented programs, some of the cable networks rose to the challenge and stayed competitive. In this regard, the overall winner in the cable realm in recent years has been HBO. It produced two outstanding shows with adult content that were also among the most popular TV programs ever—*Sex and the City*, which premiered in 1998, and *The Sopranos*, which appeared in 1999. The former, based on a memoir by writer Candace Bushnell, chronicles the professional and sexual exploits of a New York City writer named Carrie Bradshaw (played by Sarah Jessica Parker). *The Sopranos* explores the violent world of a modern organized-crime family headed by burly Tony Soprano (played by James Gandolfini).

Even while these shows were still on the air, HBO followed with more big hits, including *Six Feet Under, Band of Brothers, Angels in America,* and *Rome.* As a result, the network that had come to use the slogan "It's not TV, it's HBO" captured a

Jerry Orbach, right, and Jesse L. Martin, center, played detectives on the original Law and Order *series.*

hefty 27 percent of the entire American viewing audience in the 2005–2006 television season. Its shows also consistently won Emmys, including thirty-two in 2004 alone. Likewise, the 2007 HBO miniseries *John Adams*, featuring several great acting performances and magnificent production values, was by itself nominated for twenty-three Emmys. HBO also drew large audiences with adult-themed comedy shows, among them *Curb Your Enthusiasm* and *Real Time with Bill Maher*.

"Flowing River of Experience"

One undeniable reality emerges from these battles among the various networks for the hearts and minds of the viewing public. It is that, as both an industry and an art form, television is bigger, more diverse, more successful, and more entrenched in society than ever before. No matter what networks and shows they choose to watch, the fact is that hundreds of millions of people *do* watch their TV sets on a regular basis. In many ways they have come to rely on television, and not only for entertainment and information. As Anthony Smith puts it:

> Beneath the most routine or trivial entertainment, the [TV] medium operates as a subtle instructor. . . . It offers a continuous flowing river of experience from which we have come to draw much of the substance of our identities. Many have tried, but no one has yet succeeded, in distilling the essence of the nature of its influence, but much passes between us and television that shapes and alters us.[67]

Long ago, one of TV's pioneers, David Sarnoff, seemed to sense this momentous potential of TV to hold humanity spellbound. He said with a touch of awe, "Never before have I witnessed compressed into a single device so much ingenuity, so much brain power, so much development, and such phenomenal results."[68]

The Future of TV

The early inventors and pioneers of television had high hopes for the new medium. Yet they did not foresee either the tremendous influence it would have on society or the extensive and mystifying array of advanced technologies it would embrace by the first decade of the twenty-first century. Similarly, it is doubtful that anyone alive today can say with any certainty what TV will be like sixty or seventy years from now.

Increasingly Advanced Technologies

Based on recent trends, however, leading experts on television and the technologies allied with it have made some educated guesses about TV in the immediate future. First, they say, the medium will continue to become more technically advanced. The ongoing rise of HDTV is a good case in point. These four letters stand for "high-definition TV," which the transition to

A high-definition television set has even higher resolution and sharpness than digital TV.

digital TV has made possible. HDTV, which is beginning to catch on with consumers, is essentially digital TV with even higher resolution, sharpness, and realism than ordinary digital. "Most consumers will see a huge improvement in image quality," says one industry insider. "Consumers will also benefit from HDTV improvements such as wide-screen theater-like displays, enhanced audio quality, and new data services."[69] Most experts say that within ten or fifteen years almost all TVs in American homes will generate high-definition visuals and audio.

Also, experts predict, other advancing technologies will take television viewing increasingly outside the traditional setting of the home. Portable video devices such as cell phones, BlackBerries, and music players will be capable of receiving regular TV programming in a detailed digital format. Moreover, the TV signals themselves will, more often than not, be transmitted via the Internet. Existing cable and satellite systems, though far more advanced than earlier systems, still can carry only a limited number of channels at one time. In comparison, the Internet could potentially carry millions of channels and make selected ones available to computer users on demand. As a result, some experts suggest, more and more people will watch TV on computer screens.

Because of the many functions computers and computerized devices can perform, television will also become increasingly interactive, meaning viewers will interact in numerous ways with the networks or other TV providers in real time. This is already happening today,

for instance, when viewers phone in their votes for contestants on *American Idol* or call in to ask questions of guests on *Larry King Live.* As time goes on, viewers will e-mail the networks during broadcasts, enter chat rooms hosted by TV providers, and even upload their own homemade television programs to other TV viewers on the Internet. "If you have your own camcorder and digital edit suite," Smith points out, "you can make your own images [and] it will be increasingly possible to show them to a wider audience [of fellow TV viewers]."[70]

More Control

Another technology that is already available, often called a digital video recorder (DVR), offers a detailed guide to all available shows and allows viewers to select the specific programs they want to watch. They can then record the shows for future viewing. The first DVR system, TiVo, which appeared in the 1990s, was very successful and inspired many satellite and cable providers to institute their own DVR systems. In the near future, Laurie C. Hillstrom writes, more advanced versions of these systems will be marketed. "In addition to basic programming listings," she says,

these guides may offer advanced searching and sorting functions to help viewers find the shows they want to watch. TV listings could be embedded with tags, like Web sites, that allow viewers to search for keywords or even the names of individual cast members.[71]

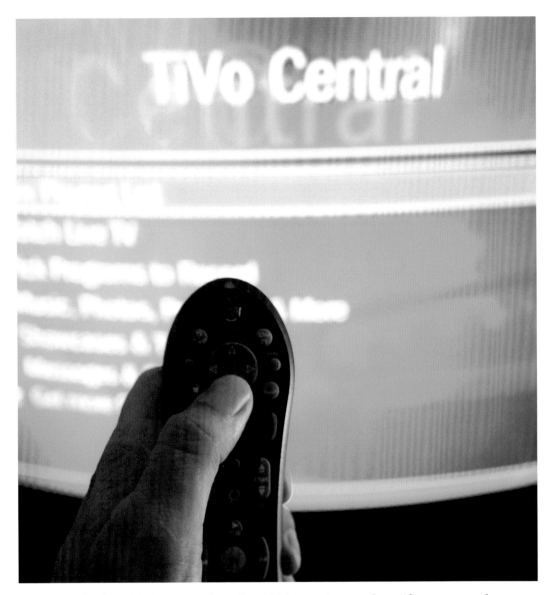

TiVo was the first DVR system that allowed viewers to record specific programs they wanted to watch.

The upshot of this and other advanced technologies on the immediate horizon is that viewers will enjoy increasingly more control over what they watch on TV, when they watch it, and how they watch it. All the experts agree that at present this trend seems inevitable. But how will the television industry and social customs change as a result of viewers having so much control? No one knows for sure, but in such a viewer-centric environment, one observer asks:

Do we still need broadcast networks? Why shouldn't all programming be delivered via cable or satellite without going through the process of network or station to home? Should people pay for each program they see in a system in which they would have unlimited choices, where they could view what they wanted when they wanted, as long as they were willing to pay for it? What would be the role of advertising then? [Finally] will the audience continue to be satisfied, or will they demand more from the medium?[72]

Only time can answer these and other questions about the future of an incredibly ingenious device that has already significantly reshaped society and will surely continue to do so.

Notes

Introduction: "The Air Has Eyes"

1. Quoted in Anthony Smith, ed., *Television: An International History.* New York: Oxford University Press, 1998, p. 1.

2. Gary R. Edgerton, *The Columbia History of American Television.* New York: Columbia University Press, 2007, p. xi.

3. Smith, *Television*, pp. 1–2.

4. Edgerton, *The Columbia History of American Television*, p. 20.

5. Carolyn Marvin, *When Old Technologies Were New.* New York: Oxford University Press, 1988, p. 3.

6. Quoted in Smith, *Television*, p. 35.

Chapter One: The Early Development of TV

7. Albert Abramson, "The Invention of Television," in Smith, *Television*, p. 13.

8. Edgerton, *The Columbia History of American Television*, p. 57.

9. Laurie C. Hillstrom, *Television in American Society.* Detroit: UXL, 2007, pp. 3–4.

10. Neil Postman, "Philo Farnsworth," *Time*. www.time.com/time/time100/scientist/profile/farnsworth03.html.

11. Years later, Farnsworth was vindi-cated. Various scientific organizations recognized his contributions and several books told the real story. See Daniel Stashower, *The Boy Genius and the Mogul: The Untold Story of Television.* New York: Broadway, 2002; Evan I. Schwartz, *The Last Lone Inventor: A Tale of Genius, Deceit & the Birth of Television.* New York: HarperCollins, 2002; and Russell Roberts, *Philo T. Farnsworth: The Life of Television's Forgotten Inventor.* Hockessin, DE: Mitchell Lane, 2002.

12. Quoted in *New York Times*, "Far-Off Speakers Seen as Well as Heard Here in a Test of Television," April 8, 1927, p. 1.

13. *New York Times*, "Far-Off Speakers Seen as Well as Heard Here in a Test of Television," April 8, 1927, p. 1.

14. Quoted in Christopher H. Sterling and John M. Kittross, *Stay Tuned: A History of American Broadcasting.* Mahwah, NJ: Lawrence Erlbaum, 2002, p. 164.

15. Quoted in Orrin E. Dunlop, "First Field Test in Television, Costing $1,000,000, to Begin Here," *New York Times*, May 8, 1935, p. 1.

16. Quoted in NBC, *Pioneering in Television: Prophecy and Fulfillment.* New York: NBC, 1947, p. 40.

17. John Western, "Television Girds for

Battle," *Public Opinion Quarterly*, October 1939, p. 552.

18. Hillstrom, *Television in American Society*, p. 46.

Chapter Two: Building a National Audience

19. Quoted in James Von Schilling, *The Magic Window: American Television, 1939–1953*. New York: Haworth, 2003, p. 73.

20. Douglas Gomery, "Finding TV's Pioneering Audiences," *Journal of Popular Film and Television*, Fall 2001, p. 127.

21. Quoted in John Lahr, "The CEO of Comedy," *New Yorker*, December 21, 1998, p. 76.

22. Edgerton, *The Columbia History of American Television*, pp. 115–16.

23. Richard Corliss, "Tuesdays with Uncle Miltie: Mr. Television, the Pioneer of a New Medium, Says Goodnight," *Time*, April 8, 2002, p. 71.

24. Philip Hamburger, "Television: The World of Milton Berle," *New Yorker*, October 29, 1949, p. 91.

25. Quoted in High-Tech Productions, "The History of Film, Television & Video." www.high-techproductions.com/historyoftelevision.htm.

26. William S. Paley, *As It Happened: A Memoir*. New York: Doubleday, 1979, p. 238.

27. Kathleen Brady, *Lucille: The Life of Lucille Ball*. New York: Billboard, 2001, p. 226.

28. Edgerton, *The Columbia History of American Television*, pp. 134–35.

29. Hillstrom, *Television in American Society*, p. 87.

30. David Rothel, *Richard Boone: A Knight Without Armor in a Savage Land*. Madison, NC: Empire, 2000, p. 193.

31. Edgerton, *The Columbia History of American Television*, p. 99.

Chapter Three: TV Becomes a Great Escape

32. Quoted in David E. Fisher and Marshall J. Fisher, *Tube: The Invention of Television*. Washington, DC: Counterpoint, 1996, pp. 305–6.

33. Quoted in Fisher and Fisher, *Tube*, p. 307.

34. Hillstrom, *Television in American Society*, p. 91.

35. Barbara Moore et al., *Prime-Time Television: A Concise History*. London: Praeger, 2006, p. 122.

36. Hillstrom, *Television in American Society*, p. 98.

37. Moore et al., *Prime-Time Television*, pp. 178–79.

38. Moore et al., *Prime-Time Television*, p. 139.

39. Maurice Gorham, *Broadcasting and Television Since 1900*. London: Andrew Dakers, 1952, p. 237.

Chapter Four: The Effects of TV on Society

40. Edgerton, *The Columbia History of American Television*, p. xviii.

41. Hillstrom, *Television in American Society*, pp. 79–80.

42. Dorothy Barclay, "A Decade Since 'Howdy Doody,'" *New York Times Magazine*, September 21, 1958, p. 63.

43. Henrietta Battle, "Television and Your Child," *Parents*, November 1949, p. 45.

44. Bianca Bradbury, "Is Television Mama's Friend or Foe?" *Good Housekeeping*, November 1950, pp. 58, 263–64.

45. Quoted in *Christian Century*, December 26, 1951, p. 499.

46. Paul Witty, "Children and TV: A Fifth Report," *Elementary English*, October 1954, p. 349.

47. Edgerton, *The Columbia History of American Television*, p. 93.

48. Aletha C. Huston et al., *Big World, Small Screen: The Role of Television in American Society*. Lincoln: University of Nebraska Press, 1992, p. 38.

49. Huston et al., *Big World, Small Screen*, p. 38.

50. Hillstrom, *Television in American Society*, p. 219.

51. Quoted in CNN.com, "Study Links TV Viewing Among Kids to Later Violence." http://archives.cnn.com/2002/HEALTH/parenting/03/28/kids.tv.violence/index.html.

52. David Halberstam, *The Powers That Be*. New York: Knopf, 1979, p. 38.

53. Edgerton, *The Columbia History of American Television*, p. 204.

54. Quoted in American Rhetoric, "Spiro Theodore Agnew: Television News Coverage." www.americanrhetoric.com/speeches/spiroagnewtvnewscoverage.htm.

Chapter Five: The Dawn of the Cable Era

55. Michele Hilmes, ed., *The Television History Book*. London: British Film Institute, 2003, p. 63.

56. Edgerton, *The Columbia History of American Television*, p. 342.

57. Moore et al., *Prime-Time Television*, p. 173.

58. Hillstrom, *Television in American Society*, pp. 107, 109.

59. Moore et al., *Prime-Time Television*, p. 198.

60. Moore et al., *Prime-Time Television*, p. 239.

61. Edgerton, *The Columbia History of American Television*, p. 400.

Chapter Six: A Channel for Everyone

62. Edgerton, *The Columbia History of American Television*, pp. 314–15.

63. Quoted in HowStuffWorks, "How Digital Television Works." http://electronics.howstuffworks.com/dtv2.htm.

64. Moore et al., *Prime-Time Television*, pp. 231–32.

65. Quoted in Parents Television Council, "Top Ten Best and Worst Shows for Family Viewing on Prime Time Broadcast Television." www.parentstv.org/ptc/publications/reports/top10bestandworst/2005/main.asp.

66. Moore et al., *Prime-Time Television*, p. 242.

67. Smith, *Television*, p. 2.

68. Quoted in Fisher and Fisher, *Tube,* p. xiii.

Epilogue: The Future of TV

69. High-Tech Productions, "Frequently Asked Questions and Information on HDTV." www.high-techproductions .com/hdtv.htm.

70. Smith, *Television*, p. 389.

71. Hillstrom, *Television in American Society,* pp. 235–36.

72. Moore et al., *Prime-Time Television*, pp. 282–83.

For Further Reading

Books

M.K. Booker, *Strange TV: Innovative Television Series from "The Twilight Zone" to "The X-Files."* Westport, CT: Greenwood, 2002. This well-informed, entertaining book examines the success of various genres and series seen as outside the mainstream of TV programming.

Gary R. Edgerton, *The Columbia History of American Television*. New York: Columbia University Press, 2007. A noted scholar of television history and lore delivers one of the best available overviews of the television art form. The reading level is high, but serious students of the subject will find it worth the effort.

David E. Fisher and Marshall J. Fisher, *Tube: The Invention of Television*. Washington, DC: Counterpoint, 1996. An absorbing, informative look at the many inventors and other individuals who contributed, in a sort of team effort, to the invention of television.

Joe Garner, *Stay Tuned: Television's Unforgettable Moments*. Kansas City, MO: Andrews McMeel, 2002. A fact-filled, entertaining look at thirty-six pivotal events in TV history.

Laurie C. Hillstrom, *Television in American Society*. Detroit: UXL, 2007. A well-researched, effective study of the rise and roles of TV in American society.

Michele Hilmes, ed., *The Television History Book*. London: British Film Institute, 2003. A collection of informative articles by noted experts about all aspects of TV history.

Mark Lasswell, *TV Guide: Fifty Years of Television*. New York: Crown, 2002. A beautifully illustrated volume with many informative articles about important TV programs and personalities from 1949 to 1999. Provides some interesting commentary about American culture during this period.

Barbara Moore et al., *Prime-Time Television: A Concise History*. London: Praeger, 2006. A well-researched, well-written overview of television genres and programming.

Anthony Smith, ed., *Television: An International History*. New York: Oxford University Press, 1998. Presents much useful information on TV history in the United States, along with detailed discussions of the television industries in Japan, Australia, and other countries.

Lynn C. Spangler, *Television Women from "Lucy" to "Friends": Fifty Years of Sitcoms and Feminism*. Westport, CT: Praeger, 2003. A thoughtful examination of women's roles in TV history.

Daniel Stashower, *The Boy Genius and the Mogul: The Untold Story of Television*. New York: Broadway, 2002. The incredible story of Philo T. Farnsworth, a key inventor of electronic television, and his struggles with TV entrepreneur David Sarnoff. Highly recommended.

Web Sites

"The History of Film, Television and Video" (www.high-techproductions .com/historyoftelevision.htm). The High-Tech Productions Web site offers this entertaining, informative time line of important milestones in these entertainment venues.

"Jackie Gleason" (www.museum.tv/ archives/etv/G/htmlG/gleasonjack/ gleasonjack.htm). This excellent overview of one of the pioneers of TV variety and comedy is part of the Museum of Broadcast Communications Web site.

"Mechanical TV: Baird Television" (www .mztv.com/newframe.asp?content=http ://www.mztv.com/baird.html). This article from the Museum of Television offers a colorful examination of the now-defunct medium of mechanical television. Follow the links to various examples and developments.

"Milton Berle" (www.museum.tv/arch ives/etv/B/htmlB/berlemilton/berle milton.htm). This article, part of the Museum of Broadcast Communica-tions Web site, tells how Berle became television's first major star.

"Philo T. Farnsworth" (www.time.com /time/time100/scientist/profile/farns worth.html). This article from the *Time* magazine Web site is an excellent brief overview of Farnsworth and his contributions to the invention of electronic television.

Television History: The First 75 Years (www.tvhistory.tv/). This Web site provides links to photos of hundreds of models of TV sets through the ages, TV museums, TV manufacturers, and more, along with some brief commentary on the evolution of the invention.

"TV's Top 125 Political Moments" (www .museum.tv/exhibitionssection.php? page=439). Follow the links in this article from the Museum of Broadcast Communications to see videos of the most-watched news events in TV history.

"TV Westerns" (www.b-westerns.com /tvwest.htm). From the Old Corral Web site, this useful, entertaining article discusses the TV Western genre, which was most popular in the 1950s and 1960s. It contains numerous links to sites detailing individual shows.

Index

Picture Credits

Cover photo: © Bettmann/Corbis
American Idol Prod./19 Television/FOX TV Network/Fremantle Media North America/The Kobal Collection/The Picture Desk, Inc., 84
AP Images, 7 (upper left, lower right), 58, 89
© Bettmann/Corbis, 17, 21, 27, 28–29, 32, 34, 40–41, 50, 62
© Mark Boulton/Alamy, 54
CBS Photo Archive/Hulton Archive/Getty Images, 57
CBS-TV/The Kobal Collection/The Picture Desk, Inc., 47
CBS-TV/NBC/Talent Assoc/The Kobal Collection/The Picture Desk, Inc., 45
© CNN/Getty Images, 69
© Corbis, 36
© Enigma/Alamy, 91
Field Mark Publications, 72
© William Gottlieb/Corbis, 14–15
© iStockphoto.com/Kirby Hamilton, 66–67
The Kobal Collection, 76
Lorimar/The Kobal Collection/The Picture Desk, Inc., 73
© Roy McMahon/Corbis, 80
National Archives and Records Administration, 6
NBC-TV/The Kobal Collection/The Picture Desk, Inc., 83
© Andria Patino/Corbis, 23
© Photos 12/Alamy, 10
© H. Armstrong Roberts/ClassicStock/Corbis, 43
Tom Stoddart/Getty Images, 7 (lower left)
Universal TV/Wolf Film/The Kobal Collection/The Picture Desk, Inc., 87

About the Author

In addition to his acclaimed volumes on the ancient world, historian Don Nardo has written and edited many books for young adults about modern history and scientific and social developments, including *The Age of Colonialism, The Great Depression, The Scopes Trial, Biological Warfare, Lasers,* and *The Search for Extraterrestrial Life.* Mr. Nardo also writes screenplays and teleplays and composes music. He lives with his wife, Christine, in Massachusetts.